Our Parents Sins Breaking the Cycle

Bernard Fisher

Our Parents Sins Breaking the Cycle
Copyright © 2021 by Bernard Fisher

Library of Congress Control Number: 2021906615
ISBN-13:   Paperback: 978-1-64398-587-9
            ePub: 978-1-64674-164-9
            Hardcover: 978-1-64674-163-2

Printed in the United States of America

LitFire LLC
1-800-511-9787
www.litfirepublishing.com
order@litfirepublishing.com

CONTENTS

PREFACE.. vii
Chapter 1   Passing of the Torch............................... 1
Chapter 2   The Biggest Illusion.............................. 5
Chapter 3   Generational Sins.................................13
Chapter 4   The Lost Generation 25
Chapter 5   The Ego... 33
Chapter 6   The Inner Child Breaking the Pattern 41
Chapter 7   Living with Awareness........................... 53
Chapter 8   Seeing Through the Illusion 59
Chapter 9   Consciously Manifesting
             the Power of Thought Word and Deeds ... 65
Chapter 10   We Are Not Alone 73
Chapter 11   Living and Creating Life as Your
             True Self.. 79
Chapter 12   Consciously Living Life with a Purpose ... 85
Chapter 13   Legacy of Love 95

THANK YOU'S

I would Like to thank the GREAT I AM ! The God of love, for lighting the way and giving me the words, wisdom, and the discipline to finish writing this labor of love

In loving memory of the first woman in my life whom I loved. You unselfishly shared your love and instilled in me the love of God. Thank you for building upon and strengthening my love of self your love continues to sustain me. I honor your life though it was short, your legacy lives on. I will always love you. You were the BEST Mom ever.

Last, but not least, I would like to thank my ancestors for paving the spiritual path for me through the expression of your lives. For I stand on the shoulders of giants and I honor and love ALL of you

PREFACE

As a child, whenever I wanted to be alone, I would go into my backyard and stare into the night sky. While gazing at the stars, I was often overcome by deep emotions, swept up in the moment, not realizing it until I felt a tear rolling down my cheek. I often had this deep sadness in my heart, feeling as if I were missing someone or someplace unknown to me. I used to think to myself, *What if there were no plants, animals, humans, earth, planets, or stars?* As I deleted all of God's creations within my mind's eye, the only thing left was darkness. I continued by asking, *What if there was no darkness? Then I would see nothing but pure white light.* Near the end of my exercise, I would think to myself, *This must be the end of God's creation, for isn't there nothing other than pure white light?*

As the years passed and I matured, so did my questions. I had a memory of being in our home, in Springfield Gardens, Queens. I came down the stairs from my bedroom and as I passed my Mother's room, I overheard her speaking to someone -- she seemed to be agitated about something. She just had an argument with my aunt, and the disagreement became intense, so she abruptly hung up the phone. As I stood in her doorway, I saw my mother with her arms raised in the air, and she exclaimed, "We used to be so close until she joined that cult religion and became a Jehovah's witness!" I must have been 12 years of age.

My response to my mother was, "Mama, what if she's correct with her choice of religion and we are wrong, being Christians?"

My mother was still in her emotions, her ego, and she probably wanted to smack me to Kingdom Hall, where my aunt worshipped. I was grateful that my mom didn't act out of her ego, but that God's grace had spared me a response that wouldn't have been favorable. She just looked at me then turned and walked away in silence. I was so relieved, and I thought to myself, there must be a God because I was saved from my mother's wrath! But within my being, I knew of the deep love and wisdom my mother had for her children, especially when we were able to respectfully express ourselves. My questions about God and life continued to increase as I grew. The more answers to my questions I received, the more I wanted to know.

My mother became a single mom again, now raising seven children. My younger brother, who would be her last child, wasn't born yet. She constantly worked to keep a roof over our heads and feed the family. She didn't have time for herself, let alone much time for her children. She was tough when necessary, and if she was stressed she never showed it, but we always felt how devoted to us she was.

We didn't grow up spending much time with my father, even though he lived nearby in the borough of Brooklyn. When my siblings and I did have the chance to spend time with him, we had to prepare ourselves to be walked all over the city. While he paraded us around, we met people to whom he had bragged about us—about our school accomplishments or other things. He would beam with pride when he introduced us to the friends of his we encountered along the way, which seemed to take us around the whole of New York City. They would compliment us, tell him how well-mannered we were, and praise our appearance. Each time after walking what seemed like half the city, we would be exhausted and vow never to visit my father again. When we did spend time with him, he would speak about life, most of the time in metaphors, and often with his style of bluntness: clarity and directness. I had no idea of the wisdom my father would pass through my unwilling ears until years later when I became a man.

The pure, untainted love we longed for from our parents would unconsciously be passed down to us in mixed forms. We sometimes received from them love with condition, deeply tainted and ruled by the ego. I wouldn't know how it affected my soul, or the souls of other family members until I decided to take the journey of discovering my parents' sins. I came to understand the power of choice and the consequences of it. How do we obtain the courage to venture into the emotional territory never explored before? As I took the road of discovery, I was unaware of the insight that would be gained about my life. All just by reaching into the lives of my ancestors, hoping to one day pass on the wisdom gained by helping others to heal their hearts and minds to be free, breaking the continuing cycle of Our Parent's Sins.

CHAPTER 1
PASSING OF THE TORCH

"Truth, like a torch, the more it's shook it shines."~William Hamilton

When I cross paths with someone, I often wonder what their life story is and how much of this story was influenced by their parents. As a child I enjoyed being around my elders; I would listen to stories or gossip (the two weren't much different) about family members, or friends of the family overcoming great challenges and difficulties, or deaths caused by mysterious illnesses. I also heard stories of cousins who could pass for being white and decided to do the unthinkable. They crossed over into white society by imitating something they were not: Caucasian. These cousins were never seen in the family again. I found it interesting to see how these family secrets still affected the storyteller; they were always spoken about in whispers, still considered taboo to openly speak of because of the embarrassment and shame it brought to the family.

When I became an adult, I observed that most families had some type of dysfunction within their tribe. I noticed that some parents were not behaving in a so-called "normal" manner; they seemed to be more emotionally wounded than others. I often wondered how one sibling could grow up having a drinking or drug problem and become abusive, yet the other siblings did not suffer from any addiction problems or become abusive? They were not exposed to any of these bad habits growing up; neither parent had any of these destructive behavioral patterns that could have led to recreational drug use or brought about abusive relationships. Then I asked myself, *How was it possible for the other children not to have any battles with addictions?* I also pondered deeply, *How could a family member suffer from depression and that depression not be rooted within the immediate or distant family going back for even two generations?*

To give another example, hypertension is genetically passed down on my mother's side of the family, mainly due to diet and stress. Her father had it and suffered from a stroke, mainly brought on by excessive drinking. Yet, he lived to the golden age of eighty-six. My mother, however, suffered a fatal stroke at the young age of fifty. Still more mystifying, her two surviving siblings have not been afflicted by this illness. When my mother passed away, not only did I want an explanation of why she died, but I was unexpectedly propelled on a pilgrimage, seeking answers to what was in my family's genetic makeup which would explain how certain genes and characteristics are passed down for generations. At that moment something within me shifted. My curiosity grew and I wondered, *What other unknown conditions were passed down from one generation to the next?* As the saying goes, "Be careful what you wish for because you just might get it," and did I ever. I was unaware that this curiosity would take me on a spiritual pilgrimage within myself, with a destination unknown, for the answers to be revealed.

Deep within my soul I heard, "Seek and you shall find," and I knew to get the answers, I had to ask the right questions—but to whom? I deciphered that I needed to go to the ones who held the keys to the doors that needed to be opened. I was open to all of the stories of my ancestor's lives from the past up to the present. It became obvious to me that I had to go to the elders in my family to obtain this knowledge. I knew that this would be difficult because quite a few family members had passed on, so there were generational gaps between those who may have the answers.

I found that there was an aunt and an uncle two or more generations away who suffered from high blood pressure or had substance abuse problems, such as drinking. I also discovered that physical abuse was also in my family history. I was surprised to find that some of these harmful matters were passed down for generations via our DNA, but only surfaced after skipping a generation or so unless activated by an unhealthy lifestyle. I began to notice within my family a genetic pattern that was switched on, physically affecting some of my siblings, but not others. Why was the gene of alcohol addictions in some and not others? I began to recall that no matter what country I was in, a random individual would approach me and strike up a conversation. With consistency, unusual occurrences would happen. These random strangers early into the exchange would speak into my life, and each one would give the same advice, "You should stop drinking." I would think to myself, *Why are they telling me this, I don't have a drinking problem?* They would continue, "God has plans for you... There's a big destiny for you to fulfill and drinking will affect the outcome." I would think to myself, *Why am I constantly receiving this warning?* The more I investigated these random coincidences, the more I began to notice that there was a deeper story unraveling, other than just carrying generational genes. I also wondered how these destructive patterns could be stopped. Then I realized that these were not only genetic patterns, but spiritual ones as well. This advanced a deeper understanding of wisdom—the revelation was that though God gives us free will, unfortunately, mankind doesn't comprehend the power of choice. These chosen possibilities will not only affect the chooser's lives in some way, but also the lives of generations to come. The generational passing of the touch comes from unconscious choice-making fueled by negative thoughts which are made from a lower vibrational level. This supports the lie of our egotistical selves about who we think we are.

The majority of the time it is shaped by the conditioning of our parent's values and societal pressures. By observing my own life, I noticed how much I was influenced by what my parents thought of themselves and how society placed judgments on race, economic classes, and gender. This made either a positive or negative impression (albeit a strong one) upon my parents' mental state, influencing their decisions in a big way. It not only affected their lives but the lives of their children. What they instilled in my siblings and I was a measuring cup filled with love and all that's the opposite of that—which is love—revealing how much love or a false sense of love from the ego that was invested into our self-esteem. When my ego was shaken by the abandonment of some kind, it triggered feelings of unworthiness, not being accepted or good enough to be loved, pushing me deeper into the lie of who I thought I truly was according to my egotistical self. Unaware that I was submerged within the cesspool of the ego, the more I believed and lived out the lie that my ego was telling me. However, I recognized that I was also carrying the sins of my parents and the cause of their choices, made from an ego-based state of mind. Unfortunately, I was unaware that I was continuously perpetuating these untruths. But to know and understand my egos untruths, I had to uncover within myself the true me. I had embarked on a path unaware that it would be the road to the freeing of my soul and the souls of future generations, giving us all liberty from our parent's sins if we so choose. For some strange reason, I intuitively knew that once I decided to go on this quest that I had to be ready and disciplined in doing the spiritual work needed, no matter what it may uncover. I knew that I had to force a way back to the core of my soul by breaking the repetitive cycle of my sins and that of my parents, ceasing to no longer believe the lie passed down for generations.

Once I decided to go on the journey to the unknown without hesitation, fear suddenly took root. It felt like I was passed a family torch that lit the way to the discovery of pieces to a family puzzle. The more the pieces were put together, the more it began to reveal a chest full of family history. A heavy load that was filled with the burdens of seven generations in the past and seven generations in the future was resting on my shoulders. I had to ask myself, *Do I want to shine the light on what so comfortably hid in the dark? What are you afraid of?* Again, my ego began to whisper in my ear all of the fears that never existed. Until the song of my heart began to play louder than the untruths of my ego. This beautiful melody told of a pilgrimage of revelations that would lead to God, the self, and love if I chose to leap with faith into the discovery and freedom from my parent's sins.

CHAPTER 2
THE BIGGEST ILLUSION

"Everything that you see is not real... But everything that cannot be seen is." —Pastor Dwayne Ramsey

I have traveled around the world and discerned many encounters numerous times along my life's path. What I've noticed is that there is a common denominator uniting all of humanity, and that's love. The desire to be loved is what all humans long to receive but yet isn't open to receiving because it's believed to be unobtainable. Why is this? To know why, we first must know what the needs of the heart are. Then if we can differentiate the longing of the heart compared to that of the ego, will we be able to accept the truth? Or will we continue to reject the answer to these questions once we discover that most of our hopes and dreams stem from our ego?

Unfortunately, the majority of humanity is unaware that most choices are made from ego-based desires. The more we choose from this place outside of love and continue to believe in this reality, the deeper we become enthralled in the illusion of life. We unintentionally, continue making decisions from the ego that it pushes us further away from truth; the authentic reality of life. But if we're accepting of this transparency, we soon will discover what the soul always knew: that there is a desire mankind longs for before their physical life ends, and that's to freely give love and to be able to receive it. Yes, I did notice other needs no matter what part of the world I was in. I noticed that everyone wanted a stable home for their family. They also desired the means to be able to bring in a constant income with access to good healthcare. One of the most important wishes is the need to be able to freely worship and perform religious practices. Depending on the country, these necessities are not available because of the inability of that governmental system to provide for its citizens. These basic needs and desires are easily obtainable for some but more difficult for the majority of the world's citizens.

The powers that be who are our world leaders of governments, banks, and the media are constantly perpetuating the lie of the ego. The lies that some are better than others because they were born into the "right" families and they inherited wealth, believing that this makes them more worthy than those less fortunate than themselves. These selected few feel destined to have the majority of the wealth. The top 3% are the ones with the power to manipulate the other 97%, convincing them to believe that they need to work to pay taxes to keep the government running, while the top 3% get away with not paying taxes that are proportional to their income, because of receiving major tax cuts. In the meantime, people are starving around the world when there is enough food for us all to eat.

This planet was perfectly created for us to forget who and what we truly are. Some souls living within this illusional world are awakening because of the spiritual work they are doing. Their spiritual practices are leading them back to remembering that they are perfect, whole, and complete beings. Souls who at one time inquired about the purpose of this life, yet having obtained some of the answers to their question by going deep within to the core of their identity. Through prayer and meditation, a soul wishes to connect to spirit by dedicating themselves to their daily practices. Hoping to free themselves from the illusion of the world by discovering that things are not what they appear to be. Like the universe and all within it, in-particular this planet, it was all created for our soul's evolution. Mankind fell out of the light by making ego-based lower-level choices absent of love. For us to remember who we truly are, we need to observe where our choices are made from. Are they formulated from an ego-based mentality? And do the repercussions of the choices made from the ego even compare to those made from love?

If we observe within our families, we will notice how the illusion of life was believed as truth, revealing how the ego was acting out and used to its fullest potential. Each parent (soul) chooses to experience and fulfill its purpose within the family soul group. These souls decided to prepare for their journey before the beginning of their physical life by utilizing their God-given right: the gift of free will. They are given the choice as to whether they will come together during their physical lives with the intent to assist in each other's soul's evolution. Fulfilling this promise is accomplished by playing the role of the father, sister, uncle, etc., having numerous interactions with family members within their soul group.

These experiences help us to evolve by allowing the purest part of ourselves to unfold as we blossom by remembering more of who we truly are; the more we remember who we truly are within this divine experience, the best we can fulfill our life's purpose. For example, a soul may come to this planet to work through not being an abusive father until that soul finds the strength to make different choices. By rediscovering his inner courage, he chooses to do the spiritual healing work necessary. Even if it requires him to go within to start to uncover the hidden emotional pain that once fueled his anger.

Continuing on his spiritual journey within, as he sifts through all the emotional pain he carried, he slowly starts to comprehend something that he was unaware of before: the discovery that he was believing in a false judgment of himself self-created by his ego within the illusional negative thoughts in his mind. Since childhood, he believed in the emotional story that the world was against him and that he would never amount to anything (continuously being told this by his parents). This unconscious self-defeating negative belief of himself is what manifested in his life. Thoughts like these, when perceived by the mind to be true, cause the emotional interpretation of these misconceptions of the self to manifest and become his reality. I searched deep within my subconscious for any false assumptions I believed about myself. Surprisingly with each discovery, it revealed more and more of who I thought myself to be within this realm of what I believed to be the reality. Unearthing that it was all a lie, it was then I realized that not only was I deceived by the illusional world of the ego, but my ancestors were also as well.

I came to understand that the physical occurrences we each are having are singular ones when it comes to the impression left by the many lessons learned from choices made along our life's journey. The experiences obtained have left a delicate impression that's uniquely catered for each soul to comprehend, created for the sole purposes of our spiritual evolution. Each soul has specific challenges it must overcome for it to grow, but each lesson is not the same. Are some souls not having this human experience born at different soul levels? Just observe the choices made by others (without judgment), and you will notice which choices are made from a higher level of consciousness compared to souls who are making lower vibrational choices. The choices made from this lower state of consciousness are done so from the ego without any recollection of who our true selves are while experiencing life in the physical. We can impact-fully change this experience by becoming aware of our light. Resulting in us not getting caught up within the illusional world. During our journey, souls often get so entangled in the illusional world that they make choices that propel them further into the darkness of the ego—further from the light which is God. As a soul ventures through the illusion, they may continue to act out by living in whatever role or title they believe best defines them. A good majority of souls may go through a few lifetimes before they start to awaken.

Some are born onto this planet possessing an awareness most souls are not conscious of. They have a clear comprehension of the truth; for example, they see clearly that their parents have lived this untruth for some time, and they want no part of it. Unfortunately, they don't know which direction to take to free themselves from it. The youth are lacking guidance and leadership from their elders. So, when a leader is missing, things fall apart—they become like lost sheep without a shepherd.

The millennial generation are acting out their frustrations, rebelling against what they are being taught by most of the educational institutions. They are being instructed on how to think in a more common practical structural way instead of in a more free-spirited individualistic manner of expression. From an early age we are taught (programmed) how to conduct ourselves within a civilized society. My mother uses to drill this decree into my sibling's and I psyche. She would command us to "act like you are civilized." So, whomever we would go visit, we were told not to be loud and that our manners must be impeccable. We would say please and thank you on cue, and God forbid if the host offered us anything to eat or drink, we were instructed to say no thank you while looking at the hot apple pies as our stomachs simultaneously grumbled loudly. I would hope that the host, who was so kind to offer, would hear our hungry stomachs begging to be satisfied. Hoping that she would insist on forcing it upon us; triumphantly satisfying our cravings by overruling my mother's objection. But our hopes and dreams were shattered by my mother's stares which were meant to remind us to not act in an unruly manner or we would suffer for the embarrassment it may cause her. Knowing what the consequences would be kept us all in line. When it came time for us to leave, my mother would get so many compliments about how well behaved we all were. As years passed, I saw how we all projected an untruthful image of the ego, an illusion of who we believed ourselves to be, and how we wanted others and the world to accept this lie.

When I traveled throughout the African continent, China, and India, I noticed in those societies that it would be considered disrespectful not to honor the elders and other cultural customs, such as not accepting something to eat or drink when offered. So, I asked myself, which societal manners and traditions would be considered civilized relative to other cultures? I needed clarity as far as what we in the west are being taught compared to what other cultures believed their truth to be. Here I was seeking transparency as an adult, imagine how confused the youths are? They are told by their elders, "Don't be a failure in life, have dreams of being successful, and dream big. Your life would be easier for you if you would just do as I say and try living life as I see what's best for you, not what you desire." Some try to do what their parents instructed them to do, but sooner rather than later, they begin to notice the validity of their elder's advice.

The youths begin to notice that it's not bringing them happiness, despite applying their parent's advice and obtaining some outstanding goals. Unhappiness came about due to them being unaware of the emotional choices of their ancestors that were hidden blocks in their lives. Also realizing that their parent's dreams may not have been what was destined for them to achieve. The powerless begin to notice that those in powerful positions around the world are not following their laws to which they are to adhere to. So, the youth ask, "Why should I believe in and follow the rules of my elders?" This confuses them because they could see that their parents were not living the truth that they preach. Instead, they were living contrary to the beliefs and visions of the life they desired for their children. Unfortunately, it's not understood by their offspring that their parents hope for their lives to be their own wishes and desires. Until one day, the elders may obtain enough clarity to be able to see beyond the illusion of their egos and begin to understand why their children were meant to have the life that was uniquely designed by the creator for them. In a Utopian society, the child's parents would understand what their soul's purpose is by recognizing their child's God-given gifts. Unfortunately, there's only a small percentage of evolved beings who are awakened enough to see through the misconception of the physical life experience. By understanding their true purpose and what it was created for, they make wiser choices knowing the consequences it would have on the lives of their children.

The millennials are driven by something deep within (though they may not be conscious of it); they feel that the illusional world is not what it could be. Intuitively, they know that it could be a much greater experience than what they have inherited from previous generations. This inner frustration is what's fueling their rebellion against the so-called norms of society. The inner drive to push back is just their true selves emerging. Subconsciously, their inner child is reminding them of who they truly are, but consciously they don't know how to be. This is the job of the elders—they are supposed to teach and nurture the youth, guiding them into the future they were born to live out, not just the life their parents prefer them to have but one God ordained them to live. By encouraging the youth to re-emerge as their true selves to be able to recognize their destiny as such, they are being giving birth to the knowledge that they have the inner strength to fulfill it. Some souls are born with an awareness of who they are. They have an understanding that their parents and most of society are living within the many lies of the ego. They recognize that their elders are so caught up in the illusional world that their soul's desire is for them to awaken to the truth. So, it constantly pushes against what's not authentic.

As I look back into my childhood, I notice how my upbringing helped solidify the collective conditioning of life's misconceptions on how we must be in the world, and this so-called norm assisted in strengthening the illusion of the lie of the ego. As an adult, I realized how I tried to be the perfect man in all areas of my life. But as time passed, deep within my soul, I felt as if I was missing something. I felt as if there was a deeper meaning to my life than what I was experiencing. In my quiet time I would ask God for clarity. I wondered, *What was I not understanding about the true meaning of my life?* After having a full day running around the city from one audition to another, from time to time during my breaks, I pondered about the mysteries of life. That night I went to bed and I had this dream. Dreams are the language of God, so receiving messages in my dreams wasn't unusual for me, but something about this dream was different. While dreaming, I noticed that the colors were much more vibrant and richer than usual. But the strangest thing of all was, as I was experiencing the dream, I felt as if the dream was the true reality. Suddenly, I woke up from the dream and as I looked around while sitting upright on my bed, it felt as if I was now existing in an imaginary world, compared to the feeling while being in the dream plane. I wondered why it happened to feel more like the truth in the dream than being in my waken state?

As I reflected on the dream I had just experienced, it brought about many more questions, so I asked God, "What must I do to live a fuller, happier life, and what's keeping me from achieving this?"

The answer He gave me was this, "To get to the root of the cause, go to the doorway that allowed entrance to finally deny it access by ridding yourself of it, through self-healing."

I then asked, "But how could I get to the place that needs the healing the most?"

Suddenly, in-between the silence, I heard the voice of Spirit say, "Reconnect with your true self; your compass to God will show you the way." At that moment, I knew that the emotional healing would help my inner child to emerge as my authentic self, remembering that it's not who my ego would have me to believe that I am. I knew that to discern the illusion of the ego, I had to go to the place within that allowed the sins of my parents to exist and the restrictions it placed in my heart and that of my siblings which needed to be healed. I understood that I needed to continue the journey that most prefer not to accept. But to understand my parent's story, I would have to go deeper into its origins.

CHAPTER 3
GENERATIONAL SINS

"The best way to hide something is to put it in plain sight."
~Author: Robert Junior

As I grew into adulthood, I would from time to time hear my mother say that the women in the family were cursed. I was curious to know why she would say that, but she wouldn't go any further with an explanation. So, I was left speculating as to what the truth was, and how much did she truly know? Her being a single parent, I wanted my mother to be happy. She was a social drinker, especially during the holidays. Mama was notorious for burning a pie or pan of the layered cakes she was baking. This was bound to happen to her as she called it, sipping on a drink, being joyous with the holiday spirit. I think the social drinking became a bit too much for her when she became a little bit too festive. As the evening progressed, she would become filled with the holiday spirit alright. Though, she didn't think so. Until her holiday ritual became a reality. The reluctant victim of her overindulgence became a slightly burned dessert, all because she had just for a few moments fallen asleep. When the following Christmas holiday came around again, we would remind my mother of her annual ritual of burning something. Of course, she would deny it with this astonished look on her face, while staring at us as if we were imagining it. But we stood strong in our condemnation of her because it was just a matter of time before the proof would come out in the baking. The holiday season was one of the most enjoyable childhood memories I have. My mom became a little girl again during the holidays, especially at Christmas. She went all out to make that day special for us all.

Occasionally I would recollect on past events, this particular memory was when I was four or five years of age. My siblings and I were returning from the engagement of a family member or friend of my mom's. I recalled my mother stumbling a little bit while trying to balance herself as she searched for the keys to the apartment. I became so upset because even at that young age, I knew that she shouldn't have been in a state of intoxication, not only for her well-being, but that of her children. As I grew into adulthood, I would occasionally find myself staring at my mom, wondering what my mother's story was. I knew within every family there was a tale. I wondered what generational saga was believed to be best suppressed and kept a secret by the elders in the family? I discovered that my mother didn't have a failed marriage and a number of unsuccessful relationships by not making the best decisions. I came to understand that most of her choices were rooted in something that was lacking in her life: love.

My mother was a very attractive woman. Occasionally I would say to her, especially on my birthday, "I'm the best thing that has ever happened to you," and she would respond by saying, "That's shit because if I had it to do all over again, I wouldn't have had you." Together we would laugh as I walked away with my chest out, beaming with pride. Because I knew in my heart that I was the one who spoke the truth; after all, it was apparent to me that she was the one in denial of the truth. When I finally woke from my egotistic daydream, I smiled because I knew that she loved me. After all, in my mind, whether my siblings knew it or not, I was her favorite for sure!

From time to time our family was hit hard with financial difficulties, but in hindsight, it had to be my mother's prayers because I often wondered how this woman, working only as a nurse's aide, could raise eight children on her own. My father from time to time would give financial support to her; it wasn't ever enough. But my mom never spoke a negative word against my father to us. My father would create little jobs for us to do so that we could have some spending money (the less he would have to give to my mom), but there was one drawback: in order to receive the money, we would have to work for it. With little assistance from my father, my mother kept a safe and stable home environment for her eight children, despite her many financial difficulties. In hindsight, I wondered how she stayed mentally and physically strong. Invariably always with a smile on her face that was so loving, even after having to discipline us. What I would soon find out about her life struggles would boost my curiosity in wanting to know how she was triumphant in overcoming some insurmountable obstacles, outcomes due to her life choices, and those of my grandparents.

My Mother's Story

I had to go back to the year 1887 to understand my mother's story. This was the year that my great grandmother, Dora Dunk, was born. She lived in the home of (I was shown a picture of a tall, handsome, high-cheekbone, full-blooded Cherokee Native American) a man by the name of Edward Thorpe and his wife, Liza. Ed's wife was barren; though they tried, unfortunately, she never was able to have children. As the story goes, my great grandmother had an affair with Ed and bore him nine children out of wedlock. Did she have much of a choice? After all, slavery had only been abolished twenty-two years prior to her birth. Besides, what power did a woman, let alone one who was black, have during that period? It was rumored that Ed's wife consented to her husband's infidelity, but that couldn't be confirmed. Great grandmother Dora lived with them in their home until she moved with her children into a house next door on the property of the father of her children.

I heard that Dora was a tough woman; she raised her children with strict rules. She ruled them with an iron fist, daring her children not to honor them. She apparently passed down her toughness and more to her daughters. My great grandmother instructed them on what they must do in order to survive. For this was her truth and what she chose to pass down to her daughters. She taught them that they needed not to be emotionally attached to a man. In order for them to get what they needed by physical means if necessary, the power was detaching from your emotions. Rather, obtaining control of the emotions of men. Whether my grandmother was mindful of what she was doing or not, this way of being was immersed in the psyche of her daughters. The male children grew up to speculate that this was how a man should be. This was all that they saw as they bared witness to their father's relationship with their mother. As adults, some of them embraced the belief that they didn't have to be in a monogamous relationship with their wives. Choosing instead to accept being promiscuous as the norm. My great grandparents continued to live in an open relationship out of wedlock. Resulting in the birth of my grandfather, Randolph, and nine other offspring born from this union.

My grandfather couldn't read or write because at an early age he had to go work on the farm. While he cultivated the land, he didn't have the time or luxury of finishing his education. As the years passed and he matured into an adult, he met and married my grandmother, Chaney Wiggins. This marriage produced eighteen children, but most of these children died during childbirth. Some were sets of twins, and some babies lived for just a few months before succumbing to an illness. Fortunately, four of the eighteen children were able to survive. Miraculously, there was a girl born; strong enough to break the cycle of death that bedeviled my grandparents for years. She was given Anna-bell. She had survived, and the birth of three more children followed.

My mother, I'm told, was born a special child. She was beautiful and smart with an inner light that shined so bright for all to see, and most did. She was a child who was content playing alone while the other children played together outside. Unfortunately, not all those who saw her light had good intentions. She was molested from the age of six to fourteen by an older uncle and two younger cousins. The older uncle orchestrated the plan while one male cousin was the lookout so that they wouldn't get caught, meanwhile the other committed the act of sexual assault. This taking of her innocence would cultivate a weak spiritual core, and this sacred foundation would be built upon during her lifetime with years of suppressed pain. This place of suffering is where my mother unconsciously from an early age and into womanhood would make her life choices from. Unsuspectingly, from this place of possibilities, it would conceivably lead her to a path that wasn't best for her. From time to time it brought her back to the pain she so desperately wanted to escape. Instead, her decisions continued to push her towards that which she ran from. This cycle of pain over time dimmed her light.

As she matured and found her voice she confided in her mother, expressing in detail what was happening to her. In those days, extended family members as well as the children lived together under one roof, making it difficult for my mother to escape from her abusers. Unfortunately, my grandmother chose to say nothing. I assume my grandfather wasn't aware of his daughter's violation, so life continued on as usual. Unfortunately, my grandmother's decision to keep this family secret to herself would have major consequences. It would leave a spiritual stain that would not only encompass my grandmother's soul, but the lineage of future generations of women was impacted in a major way. This must have devastated my mother, causing her to inwardly withdraw from her family. The first chance she would get, she would leave them. My mother married at an early age. She got married to escape the abuse and the disappointment from the lack of support she received from her family, especially from the one she confided in. (Incapable of knowing what the future held, she probably never thought that this would be her only husband by marriage.) My mom may have believed that she was escaping the sexual abuse inflicted upon her by relatives, unfortunately, that pushed her into another abusive relationship that came in the form of a marriage. That union produced two children, my two eldest sisters, Peggy and Selma Jeanette. But that wouldn't stop her. Soon my mother would take flight again with the hope of a better life by getting out of another bad situation. But this time it was not only to save herself, but to provide a better environment for her two young children.

In search of a better life, she was now a single parent who had to provide for her family back in the south. In those days, there weren't many opportunities in rural North Carolina, let alone being a young, single parent raising two children. Blacks at that time migrated north to the big cities for better opportunities. So, my mother decided to leave the country life for better opportunities up North. She left not only her husband, but also her two children with her parents and moved to New York City. My sisters were left with my grandparents while my mother went in search of better opportunities, freedom, and possibly love up North. My sisters were raised by my grandparents for 8 years before my mother got herself situated with work and a home and sent for her children. But when the time came for her to be reunited with her two daughters, a third child was born from a short-term affair; my sister, Sharon (my mother would withhold the true identity of my sister's father well into my sister's adult years. Sharon was told that my father was her biological parent). My sisters Peggy and Jeanette were sent from North Carolina up to New York City to join their newborn sister and mother in Brooklyn, New York. By then my mom had started a new relationship with what would soon become my father.

My mother and father's union lasted for seven years. When they separated, I was three years old, and the sixth child of seven birthed by my mother. When they separated, my father continued to live in Brooklyn. By good fortune, my mother moved the family out to the suburbs a year later into what would be the first house that we would live in. We were moved by my mother's new boyfriend, and they were expecting the arrival of a baby boy; this would be my mother's eighth and last child. We moved to a middle-class neighborhood in Laurelton Queens. This was the first house we had ever lived in. It was a small, two-bedroom house, made into a three-bedroom. With the arrival of my little brother, Robert Junior, we needed more living space. Though the house was small, it was a big step up from a one-bedroom Brownstone apartment, made to accommodate a growing family.

The house in Queens was a small yellow and white house, surrounded by well-kept middle-class homes. We had a milkman who delivered free milk at our doorsteps. I guess this was, in a small way, a luxury my mother financially sacrificed for. After all, she still had a little country girl in her being raised on a farm. The dining room was converted into the master bedroom, but after a while, even that wasn't enough to accommodate eight growing children. So, my new younger brother's father, Robert Earl, moved us into one of the homes that he owned with his cousin that had become available from previous tenants. After living in the small house in Laurelton for two years, the three-bedroom converted into a four-bedroom house felt like a mansion. Our new home had a porch, two huge trees in the front yard, and many more in the back. We had apple and wild berry trees—my mom would later plant a vegetable garden. This would be our last move; in this house we would all mature into adulthood until we ventured out into the world.

Over the years, we would occasionally see my father for graduations or when he had to give us money, though most of the time he had my siblings and I go to his place to work for it doing odd jobs. Each time when it came time for us to depart, my father wouldn't allow us to leave without him lecturing us about life and its many lessons. Numerous years passed, and we were all young adults except my younger brother who was only seventeen and entering his last year of high school. Not long before my mother's passing, my father wanted to reconcile his dissimilarities with my mother with the hopes that they may possibly rekindle their relationship. But my mother had no interest in that offer. She thought it was amusing because all of the hard work of raising her eight children, four of which were his, had already been achieved. My mother had previously decided to give us all the same last name of her first and only husband by law: Fisher. She said that she made this decision because she did not want all of her children to have different last names (I guess to save us and herself from the embarrassment of having to explain our different fathers). Making that decision made it much easier for us to grow up with the same last name; she said it was nobody's business to question who our fathers were. We were all raised to be brothers and sisters, not half-siblings. Later in life I started to notice certain generational characteristics and genetic patterns amongst my brothers and sisters. This piqued my interest to find out where these unusual habits and specific peculiarities came from.

My Father's Story

My father's family came from Mississippi, they moved from the South up to the Northeast, New York City. They too migrated up North in search of better-paying jobs with the dream of having a much better future than what Mississippi could provide. My parents met in New York City, years prior to their meeting my father's story was still being written. One day he and his brothers and sisters were informed by their father that their mother was going to the hospital. They had no idea that this would be the last time that they would ever see her again. Unbeknownst to them, their mom was taken to a mental institution for rest, but she unfortunately had a nervous breakdown. When my grandfather, Abe, returned home after committing his wife into the hospital, he never spoke to them again about their mother's (who had died in the hospital) condition. It was rumored that she perished on the operating table because the doctors who performed the operation mistook their mother for another patient (today that would be considered malpractice). It's rumored that the physicians experimented on her, the mystery of her death is still a paradox to this day.

When my father reached adulthood, he married his first wife at the age of 21. This union would bring into the world two children. Not too long after, tragedy would strike my father's heart again as his wife would succumb to an untimely death. I was encouraged to try to understand my father's psyche with the aid of my cousin, Joseph, who was a social worker and a pastor. He helped me to recognize where the inception of all my dad's pain came from. Joseph helped reveal that my father and his siblings weren't given an explanation that would have given them closure to the many questions they may have had about the death of their mother. I began to identify my father's pain, the source that may have caused him to emotionally retain his abandonment issues. Later in life, I would recognize that I too was carrying unconscious pain concocted in my mind as a child. A consequence of my parent's separation and my father's lack of guidance that was consistently absent over the years.

I wasn't mindfully aware that I felt rejected by my father, or that it was emotionally affecting me to develop abandonment issues. I became conscious that I wasn't fully open with my emotions, especially within loving relationships. Some of my friendships were also unbalanced, I felt that the trust and respect that was given by them wasn't sincere. Being in the entertainment industry, most relationships were based on what they could get out of what they thought I had, instead of defining the relationship on who I truly was. Though it was recognizable to me, I chose not to accept the truth that I knew, and I didn't question what I was shown. Being in my ego, I thought that it was petty and that it wasn't my problem if they felt insecure. I was so preoccupied that I kept unknowingly putting myself into abandonment situations. Causing in time some relationships to become unbalanced because I would limit the love I gave to my woman. I established relationships that were destined to abruptly come to an end.

I was told that my parents had a very loving relationship in the beginning until outsiders, be it family or friends, caused problems between them. Fused with the unconscious emotional problems within themselves, my parent's relationship was foreordained to fail. I was four years of age, and my youngest sister, Michelle, was two. My parent's union had added another four children, giving my mother the responsibility of caring for seven children. It was obvious that my father favored my eldest brother, Jeffery, and Michelle, and that was ok with my brother Anthony and I. Whenever my father and I did get together, our personalities would often clash. I would always see my father's faults, and I would respectfully make it known to him how I felt about them. As I matured, I always would seek wisdom and understanding after acting out in my ego, though, I wasn't yet aware of my ego at that time. I would continue to pursue discussions with others; sometimes I would go to visit my cousin Carolyn and her husband, Joseph, seeking their spiritual wisdom. I was able to go deeper into my father's pain—they guided me to see that my father did not know how to love or be loved because of his traumatic childhood experience with his mother and the sudden death of his first wife. These early life traumas caused my father to slowly close his heart instead of opening to love. My grandfather never gave my father the psychological assistance that he and his siblings needed to cope with the abandonment they must have felt.

I later discovered in my adult years that I unconsciously put myself in abandonment situations a lot, this having to do with my father's sins. These choices were made from suppressed pain and abandonment. Generational pain that would unconsciously become a repetitive cycle until I became mindful of where I was choosing from. This self-reflection helped me to recognize the feelings of desertion which resulted in my father not being able to freely love. I imagined the abandonment my mother must have felt when my grandmother didn't openly support her the way that she wanted. Instead of withholding the violation committed against their child and disclosing it to my grandfather, My grandmother chose not only to keep the secret; but she also didn't cast out the family members who committed the assault against their daughter. Instead life continued on as usual and it was never spoken about again.

I came to understand that the decision of my grandfather not to discuss the passing of his wife with my father and his siblings affected them long-term because they weren't given the psychological or spiritual support from my grandfather. He also didn't get that loving support from his parents, and so on. This set them on a path of making fear-based life choices backed by grief and the lack of feeling loved and protected. In the circumstance of my mother, my grandmother's choices continued to propel generational sins, passing them down to the next generation. I not only observed and experienced how their life choices affected my life, but also the lives of my siblings, and that of my nieces and nephews.

In 2015, I went to the funeral of my father's sister Naomi to pay my respects. It was the first time in years that I had seen my father's family. A few years prior when he had passed away, I didn't attend my father's funeral. I happened to be in Mozambique, and I didn't have much of a longing for my father to go. So here I was, at his sister's funeral, sitting and scrutinizing the relationships my father had with his children. If it wasn't for Naomi pushing and guiding my father to have a relationship with his offspring, who knows what kind of a connection we would've had. I wasn't concerned about what my father's side of the family might say about me, considering that I did not attend his home going (funeral), and I didn't really care. Deep within, I knew that I had questions about my father's life with his family that needed to be answered.

My father's youngest brother, Raymond, gave me some of the answers to the questions that I seeked. My uncle told me that he and his siblings did not know which story to believe. The one I recalled was that his mother was mistaken for another patient, so the doctors operated on my grandmother and she didn't survive, or that they intentionally did experimental surgery and she died on the operating table, due to doctor's error. That explanation surprised me because I hadn't expected to hear that theory, but I was really taken aback by my uncle's word after sharing that story with me.

He said, "My mother left me when I was three years old, I am the baby of all my siblings, and everyone comes to me for answers. Just because a man [his father] remarries another woman after an experience like that, doesn't mean that the stepmom would treat the children as her own." Uncle Raymond continued, "My brothers and sisters and I were not raised to be close, I was lucky to be raised by my mother's sister, but I kept at a distance from my aunt's love, though, I was grateful. I never wanted to have children, but I have four now, each with two different women. The wife I have now just wants me for my money."

There was a short silence between us; I was surprised by what I was hearing because this seventy-plus-year-old man had just regressed to a wounded little boy. I said with a smile, "You're just like my father, your brother."

He continued to speak, "When I asked Kim's [his daughter] mother for her hand in marriage, her mother belittled me. She said that her daughter was a well brought up child, that her daughter could not marry me. I couldn't understand how I was not good enough for her daughter, but her mother would soon find out that her daughter wasn't that proper, she was already pregnant at that time." As he told me his truth, I thought to myself, *How could this man, my father's brother, still be so emotionally wounded at his age? And what impact had it had on my cousins, his daughters, and grandchildren?*

While listening to my father's brother, I could still feel and hear the pain in the words he spoke, even after so many years. As I continued listening to his story, his voice faded in the distance and my inner thoughts were more prominent in my mind. I heard my thoughts say, *This man that stood before me, at the age of seventy-four, was still carrying around so much deep pain. This suffering kept him from loving himself and being loved by others. Instead, he chose to not get close to anyone.* I had an epiphany that all can be traced back to the abandonment of his mother, and father who detached himself from the needs of his children.

As I came back from my inner thoughts, my uncle was still talking, "I don't know anything about my father's family." A thought came to me as I listened to my uncle speaking his truth, *I didn't know that much about my father's dad's family.* He continued, "I don't know what town they came from, only the state, Mississippi." I was taken aback by my father's brother's last statement, "The sins of the father are passed down to the children."

I was dumbfounded by what I had just heard. I looked at him and said, "This is the subject of the book I am presently writing." My father's last two remaining brothers just sat there in silence. As we continued to remain in the stillness my uncle's had created while simultaneously reflecting on my thoughts, I began to slightly shake my head. In my mind I repeatedly heard, *The sins of our parents are passed to the next generation, and that's destined to contribute to their displacement.*

CHAPTER 4
THE LOST GENERATION

"The youth don't have faith in themselves because they lost faith in their elders"—Spirit

I began to have many questions about life. My inquisitiveness about the many experiences I was having while being on my life path increased my curiosity of trying to understand life's mysteries. There were quite a few times when I felt as if I was unable to find my way. I didn't know how I emotionally felt about my life. I may have been seen on television, films and magazines, or while traveling to and from different countries. This would be a charmed life for some, I thought, so I asked myself, why was I not totally happy? At times I felt spiritually lost and lonely, but I could not understand why. This brought about a strong desire to get answers to my many questions, so again I brought them to God and waited for the answers.

A familiar thought came to me: in order to receive the answers to my questions, I had to ask specific questions with clarity. I wanted to know why I was repetitively making the same mistakes. It wasn't until I was reminded to go within, so I meditated, and it was revealed that most of my dysfunctions and pain were the consequences of my choices. I had repetitively made the same lower-level choices that were connected to an accumulation of generational sins that weren't atoned for or healed by my ancestors. Unfortunately, their sins were passed down for many generations, right up to the present; the consequences of their choices were still becoming a burden for my siblings and I to have to carry. My ancestors, I am almost certain, weren't aware that their choices would influence or affect the lives of many generations along their bloodline. This resulted in my siblings and I believing in a false sense of self, causing us at times to have no confidence in ourselves or the society in which we lived. This unconscious acceptance of emotional suffering caused some to physically act out, or develop self-doubt and bitterness. It resulted in some to drink and to self-medicate themselves so that they wouldn't have to deal with their emotional burdens. This induced some to develop addictions of numerous kinds. Not realizing that these emotional hang-ups were continuously showing up, oftentimes we unconsciously reacted from the place of our ego where we felt most comfortable. Unfortunately, in this space our emotions ruled, and we would unleash the emotional fury upon those we felt hurt or angered us because they deserved it. I thought about the many instances when I was ruled by my emotions and reacted in a manner filled with so much rage, and once the anger subsided, I would blame it on others and continue on with my life until I experienced a similar situation that would again trigger my ego. I would repeat this occurrence without ever attempting to understand where this anger was coming from until I got tired of the repetitive cycle of getting caught up in unwanted confrontations. This raised internal questions like wondering what was triggering my outburst. I recognize that the emotional anger I gave to others—though in my egotistical mind they may have been at fault, even though I desperately tried to avoid the confrontation—my actions became emotional blocks in my life, inflicting me with invisible wounds that needed to be healed.

I became mindful of what I did to others. Those wounds hindered my choices, influencing them most of the time in a negative way. I recognized that when our minds are not clear due to painful experiences that are difficult for us to let go, this clouds our psyche with negative impressions. This provokes us to make irrational choices that continue to impede our lives. This repetitive cycle needed to come to an end, but how? I felt lost; I wasn't sure of a clear resolution because both of my parents were deceased. Then it came to me: if I could reveal how I was influenced by my parent's life experiences and that of previous generations, I may obtain a clear understanding of the contributing factors of how my ancestor's intentions influenced my choice-making?

The conditioning came from previous generations' unfulfilled dreams and desires that assisted in molding their self-confidence, or lack thereof. This affected their faith in the love they had not only for themselves, but others. This resulted in their belief in love to be tainted in a positive or negative way, prompting their life choices to be rooted in love (God), or in self-pity (ego). Most of the societal choices will be made from the ego. This seed will continue to blossom into the lives of their children, their children's, children and so on, until a soul is born into the family, strong enough to see through the repetitive societal traps that are littered within the family's dysfunctions. When I became aware of the dysfunctions within myself and the root of my dysfunctional behavior, I began to notice it in humanity as well. I became aware of the younger generation, or should I call them, the lost generation; the youth of today are lost and angry because of it.

Their souls are broken because they have no faith in their elders, and this has caused them to lose faith in themselves. You can see their inner turmoil by just watching or reading the news. Social media has become their mentors, replacing the role of their parents. Why learn from their parent's years of instructing when they can quickly gain understanding by watching a tutorial, podcast, or someone's masterclass online? The millennials are living in the world of internet access, everything is at their fingertips, spending more time locked into becoming or creating the next hottest thing. They are spoiled with being able to purchase merchandise that's delivered the next day. Some are starting companies, socially connecting and dating online—their lives revolve around the internet. The majority haven't taken a moment to nurture a relationship with Spirit. However, they spend more time playing video games and staying mentally and physically occupied than dedicating some time to reconnect with their true selves. So, there's no surprise that they are venting out their frustration all over social media until one day it's acted out within their homes and public.

Like the two mass shootings that recently happened in San Antonio, Texas, and Ohio. A divide has developed between parents and their children, the information age has taken the place of their elders or those in a position to help by becoming a bridge from the intellect back to the heart.

Families are no longer coming together as a group united in love. One reason for this is due to them not making an effort to spend more time together. Family time is more often spent with themselves because of the different work and school schedules. The youths are becoming less social because of easy access to the internet that's connecting them to all of the social media sites, video games, and dating apps, not leaving much time for them to socially connect. One reason for this is due to them constantly playing video games causing them to become social media dependent. The number of likes and followers they have, the more socially accepted they feel. This is causing generations to drift further apart, deeper into a more ego-driven generation that's becoming a consumer-driven society.

The age of technology connects us to a vast amount of edited and unedited information making it difficult to differentiate from what's true or false while being kept abreast of what's happening around the world in real-time. The youth are being bombarded with negative information causing them to lose a sense of self. This results in them becoming disillusioned with the world and its leaders. Subconsciously, they are in search of direction, someone to be the light, to guide them with truth and love. This is why there is an increase in them joining gangs, engaging in drug use, and early sexual experiences. This is influencing their hopes of becoming more promiscuous like reality TV stars and emulating what they see on porn sites by having easy access to it.

The youth have so much pent up anger and disappointment that they are bringing it into the schools, releasing it by acting out. On social media, kids are being bullied by posting untruths about another student they may not like. This is adding more harm to that person suffering with more lies, causing some to feel that the only way out of their misery is by committing suicide. Teachers and parents are also becoming victims of this suppressed anger, some of the youth seem to have stopped dreaming. I believe a big portion of the problem is because they are living in the world of instantaneous information resulting in the dulling of their senses. This causes a deeper disconnect from Spirit, impeding them from reconnecting and experiencing their inner child true selves. Instead, they attach deeper to a false sense of self: the ego. Millennials are missing moral leadership; the majority are not being guided or nurtured by functional parents or elders within the community. If parents could get through to them, they could aid in the healing of their children's minds by urging them to go within to the source of the pain. Instead, the youth doubt themselves, they have no trust in society because of broken promises, and a lack of support from the previous generation not investing in their future. So, they don't have the desire to even try to go within to gain an understanding of themselves. However, when they do receive love and support, they tend to doubt it because they have lost faith in their elders and those in leadership positions.

What future does humanity have living within the world of the ego? Starting with the belief of separation, a false belief is that humanity is alone on the globe. Today's youth perpetuate this lie with the assistance of social media. Today they have instantaneous access to so much information at their fingertips as it's all just a Google away, and unfortunately, most of the content that's on the web promotes anger and fear. Even dating is created to be much more convenient, all you have to do is go to someone's profile, and if you have a few things in common or are attracted to the person's photo, all you have to do is send a request for a date. If you receive a response back accepting your request, he or she may slot you in for a date on Wednesday. Meanwhile, they have a date on the remaining days of the week with others, all made possible by accessing their bio page from their smartphones. Press a button and a date is made, it's as simple as that. Dating has been made so manageable without having to leave the comforts of their home, saving them time and the inconvenience of having to socialize in-person to meet someone.

There are those that argue that having so much easy access to information from the worldwide web is destructive. It's said to be a major contributing factor in the breaking down of society's moral values, nudging a generation to become much more promiscuous at an early age and causing them to participate in some of the most deviant sexual acts. That's becoming the norm; they're becoming numb to it. I recall at age twenty-two, I was trained as a volunteer for the Family Court of Nassau County. I was unaware that I had developed a good reputation as a volunteer and was offered employment to create a mediation program, counseling, and training the students at Roosevelt High School. I was warned by the faculty of the school to keep the doors open while speaking to a female student or have a male student around as a witness, just in case I'm approached and propositioned by a female student. I couldn't understand why I was being warned daily about this until one day I overheard some of the students talking about their sexual escapades; it made my jaw drop. I thought back to how I learned about sex because I grew up in a fatherless home, I realize now that what I thought I knew then and how I learned it was primitive compared to that generation. Today's world has become smaller because of the worldwide web. We are able to get information instantly. We can study online to obtain a degree without ever having to step foot on a college campus. It's not difficult to start your own business and work from home. Now that we are experiencing a pandemic, graduations and anything that has to do with socializing has all been put on hold. Until we are able to find a cure for COVID19, how will this socially affect a generation that was already becoming socially inept. The millennials will hold the power to the future of technology. What will they do with it? How can they keep themselves from repeating the mistakes of the previous generation without proper guidance and trust in their elders? The choice is theirs to make. Will it be used for good to produce a better life, or a destructive one?

We seem to have lost touch with everyday social contact with family and friends. The basic human connections with one another are scarce; everyone seems to have created a self-centered world of their own. This generation seems to have lost the freedom of having and expressing their own opinions. Instead, they are allowing themselves to be programmed by watching and listening to a not-so-well-rounded partisan news and radio stations. Furthermore, they are permitting themselves to get caught up in the fantasy lives of their favorite music artists or reality show stars. This keeps their minds preoccupied in the illusional world, preventing them from going within to do the soul work so badly need.

I have a saying, "God always sends me somebody," from when I was living an unconscious life within my ego. I was traveling the world, making lower-level choices, partying, and socially drinking, all which impaired my judgment. The attractive women I met were a dysfunctional mirror of myself at the time. They were just searching for love, no matter in what form (mostly physical) it came in. Nevertheless, there was always someone, or something, that pulled me out of the darkness back into the light. I could have been sitting in a park in London, eating in a restaurant in Paris, walking down the street in Milan, strolling with a friend along the beach in Cape Town, but this time I was sitting in the barbershop in downtown Brooklyn and the only woman amongst the men in the barbershop said to me, "May I touch your hand?" As she held on to it while looking directly into my eyes she said to me "You're a beautiful soul," and she began to speak into my life that only my heart of hearts was seeking answers to.

The beautiful thing about those moments was the souls I happened to cross paths with. They became vessels for God, and through the sharing I was able to discern messages from a total stranger that only I could confirm. I was always left with a reminder that I was loved. Each and every time I knocked myself out of the light into the darkness due to choices that were made from acting out in my ego and not from my true self.

The creator who was always with me sent souls of his choosing, if not for a reason, a season, or a lifetime. They came into the darkness to drop a jewel of light, illuminating the way by reminding me of who I truly am and always shall be. Their wisdom helped me to see clearly through life's illusions, guiding me back into the light. We all have to be there for someone if called, especially now more than ever before, for the lost generation is crying out: "How do we free ourselves?" By going deep within the depths of our soul to heal our true selves. Reconnecting with the inner child (our compass to God) is one way I believe that we will lead not only ourselves but the lost generation back to our highest truth. By reconnecting to the self, we are reconnecting to the "source"; the source of all of creation, the force of God within that can lead all generations out of the dark and back to the light of love.

CHAPTER 5
THE EGO

"Why would you live in the ego? The ego doesn't know love, it can't filter it… Nor can it identify love."—God

When we are born into this illusional world through the womb of forgetfulness we are given free will—the choice to have this human experience by falling from grace. The grace of knowing that we are perfect, whole and complete beings, created from the source of our existence, which is the highest truth. Our fall from love was so that we could experience what it's like to live in the world of the ego. A realm where the alter-egos selfishness is used as the best warfare against reconnecting back to the highest consciousness which is love. During our life experience the ego will be one of our most formidable nemesis' preventing us from remembering who we truly are. While experiencing life on this earth plane the ego will be masked in a world made up of many illusions. If you want to observe the pressures and the effects of the ego, just take a look at planet earth. Presently in today's current events, 130 people were shot and killed in Paris by Muslim extremists who believe that they are killing for a greater purpose. Causing Syrian refugees to risking their lives seeking safety in another country. Just to have a chance at a better life so their children no longer have to see bloodshed. Due to the bombs and terror of extremists who believe that they are fighting a holy war in the name of Allah.

Presently in the United States, President Trump is attempting to pass laws advising government officials and agencies not to accept refugees of a lower economic and social class, or groups that are from non-European countries. This is another way of warning the refugees that there's no need for them to apply for asylum because there're not desirable. Political candidates are running to represent their party with the hopes of becoming the next leader of the free world. Yet the current serving President of the United States, Trump, says things daily that are so divisive and hateful that it seems that he has no compassion for others. The more outrageous the comments, the higher he hopes his poll numbers and crowd size at his rallies may increase. He uses fear-based rhetoric, and he bullies anyone who exposes his lies and weaknesses. Trump purposely perpetuates his lies with one goal in mind, and that's to create fear and divide the American people for selfish reasons.

This may cause other countries to follow the United States and tighten, if not close, their borders causing their citizens to develop *us* against *them* mentalities. But how can humanity not care when there are starving children and families around the world that could be easily fed? If only those who are able to help would just let go of their selfish ways and come together as one to help those in need. Imagine how quickly this problem could be resolved by successfully leaving no hungry mouths begging for assistance. Furthermore, the planet is being stripped of all of its natural resources so fast that mother nature can not replenish herself at the rate in which it's being depleted. Look at how we are poisoning the clean water, it has become undrinkable, like what's happening in Michigan and now parts of New Jersey. Our selfishness is killing our wildlife on land and sea. Humanity is eating in large quantities genetically modified foods promoted by world governments who have no intention of going back to organically produced foods. It's not lucrative enough for them to produce. This is creating consumers who have no desire to change their eating habits, so why would consumers change their produce habits when unhealthy food is sold at a much cheaper price compared to organic food? Foods that promote a much healthier body, not one that's destined to become dependent on medication? Could this be the reason why the FDA is promoting genetically modified foods? This is resulting in big financial profits for pharmaceutical companies.

This has become a materialistically driven world, unconsciously determined to fulfill its main purpose, and that's to satisfy the ego. This keeps us preoccupied with wanting to have all of the latest trendy merchandise, just to be envied by family and friends. Our ego drives us to imagine that if you wore the best clothes and drove the most expensive cars, it has to be parked at the largest home. Not to mention having the hottest companion next to you with an attractive face and an amazing body. Then, and only then, will I be happy and successful—if I was rich? There are many in society who believe this to be so, creating societies that have become so self-absorbed, cultivating an ego-based mentality. This selfish way of thinking propels us deeper into the many forms of the ego, further away from our true selves: love. All that the ego is not.

This absence of love is causing nations and those with power, prestige, and wealth to not be concerned about the underprivileged. So, if the cries of the less fortunate are not heard by the privilege, who will listen? Unfortunately, the egos of those who are in a position to help may cause them to turn a deaf ear and a blind eye towards the less fortunate, all because of greed. Unfortunately, all they want is more of what they already have. By continuing to endorse this narcissistic behavior, it causes them not to develop emotions and encourage the ones that need assistance the most. This egocentric selfishness transpires within a lot of families as well, turning family members against each other.

The ego-driven person will never be happy or fulfilled because the ego is never satisfied. It wants to obtain more and more, by any means necessary, and it only cares about a false sense of self. Though the ego has disdain for everything that doesn't cater to its selfish needs, we should not want to wish destruction upon our ego, even if our desire is for it to go away. After all, it's just fulfilling a purpose within God's creation. The main objective of the ego is to keep us distracted with drama. The more we act out these untruths, the more it continues to support the fallacies on the earth plane. This becomes an impediment, preventing humanity from awakening to its true essence within. This is achieved by keeping our minds busy with negative thoughts that trigger our beliefs about someone or something. Instantaneously, an emotional response is rendered, fueled by negative energy which enables the manifestation of unfavorable experiences. If you have thoughts of the inadequacy of not being good enough, unloved, or illnesses, then these negative feelings may cause us to lash out in anger, projecting it towards others and possibly harming ourselves. Our self-hatred may stem from our feelings of unattractiveness because we aren't happy with our bodies. These thoughts brewing in our minds manifest into our physical lives causing some to become obese, resulting in other biological and mental illnesses, as well as developing emotional baggage that we may carry throughout our lives. If it's not healed, our dysfunctional feelings toward ourselves could develop into an egocentric view of self, possibly influencing the youth by passing it down to the next generation. Once they become adults, they may continue to eternalize the lie of the ego by causing parents to dump fear into their children's psyche., conditioning them to become selfish, insecure, and giving rise to them having no love of self. This supplies their egos with more dysfunctional emotional power, in addition to the generational sins of their parents; blocks that another generation will have to overcome.

We should be grateful that during our descent into this physical pilgrimage that God did not forsake us during the fall from grace. Instead, he left us with guides to do his bidding in assisting us with recalling our true existence. If it was not for the ego showing us who we are not, we wouldn't know who we truly are. We were sent many teachers to help us to awaken, but most souls will not hear the creator calling for his children to awaken from this illusional world before returning back to the light. The way back is by reconnecting to our inner child true selves, our campus to God. With the assistance of our Angels and guides protecting us and showing us the way, throughout our many trials and tribulations. Our inner child is everything that the ego is not, reminding us that we are perfect, whole and complete beings of pure unconditional love. Moving towards the place of devotion, if only we are able to listen in-between the silence and hear God guiding us out of the darkness back into the light. What is this darkness that we all need guidance out of? It's a place where love does not lodge but lower-level consciousness does, an environment where separateness and selfishness coexist. Lower-level minded people are constantly having thoughts like, "I must look out for myself if I'm going to survive in this cold, hard world because there isn't enough for everyone where only the strong survive."

Residing in the world of our ego, it masterfully manipulates us into believing that we are separate from others, even amongst our family. We are compelled to believe that we are living in a world of lack because there seems to not be enough love in the world. You can see examples of this by listening to family members' responses after hearing their cell phone ring, noticing that it's a brother or sister calling, and you hear, "Why are they calling? They just want to borrow money—I'm not going to answer."

I've also heard people say, "My family is so dysfunctional that I can't be bothered with the drama." Maybe the brother or sister that called wasn't calling for money. Perhaps they just needed a listening ear that they could talk to? Or they called only to hear your voice, to tell you that they love you. We should ask ourselves, where do these deep wounds of anger come from?

To find the answers, we have to look deep within the pain, and the answer will be revealed. For example, a woman that's physically beautiful with the intellect to match, to others she may appear to be perfect with the confidence they wish they had. But to that woman in her mind, she believes herself to be the opposite of what others physically see. Deep within, she's not happy with what she sees, but unfortunately, she only feels as good as the attention she gets. I've seen this many times when I was modeling.

I had a buddy of mine at the time who was suffering from the effects of having low self-esteem. Meeting him for the first time and seeing his outward appearance, you would have never thought of him having any insecurities. His physical stature seemed to be perfect; he was a blond, six foot tall, well-built guy who plays three different sports. Not to mention that he's very articulate and able to speak to anyone. Total strangers would tell him that he looked like a superhero.

Everywhere he went he got stared at; people would approach him to ask if he was someone famous because they thought that they had seen his face before. One day he came to my place, sat on my couch and asked "Bernard, why do I long for intimacy from a woman, and if I don't have it, I don't feel good enough?" My response to him was that if he could only see himself the way others saw him, that question wouldn't be asked. This was the beginning of many sessions guided by Spirit. Mike discovered that when he was a child his mother had a volatile marriage with his father, and when they divorced, she mentally disconnected from her children. His mom didn't have a desire to live. She became dependent on prescription drugs and fell into a deep depression. The more she medicated herself, the more she slept. His mother would kick him and his two siblings out of the house very early in the morning each day. He said most of the time they didn't have food to eat. Mike recalled that there were days that he would lay in bed watching a basketball game while drinking a half-gallon of milk. Some days that would be his only meal because his mom wouldn't allow them to come back into the house until later that evening. There were days that he and his siblings would wait after school for his mom to pick them up, but she never did. He explained that his parents never showed up to any of his games. When the game ended, he watched the parents of his teammates pull up to drive his friends home; he would have to walk for miles, even during the winter months, to get home.

Mike recalled that whenever his mother would hear him and his brother and sister laughing and having fun, she would separate them by leaving him in the front yard, placing his twin brother in the back of the house, and his sister was taken inside of the home with her. He felt that his mom separated them because she didn't like to hear them having fun when she felt miserable. He disclosed to me that both his parents would constantly tell their children that they were worthless and that they would never amount to anything. He and his siblings continued to hear these negative things said to them well into their adult years. At that moment, Mike had an epiphany that he never developed a love for his mother—the Oedipus complex was never fully developed (the Freudian theory). They never formulated a healthy, nurturing, relationship between them when he was a child. Now, as an adult, he longs for the deep intimate feelings from a woman—the closeness he didn't receive from his mother.

Mike began to recognize how this affected him in other areas of his life. Whenever he got close to achieving his goals, he would sabotage his dreams by acting out in repetitive, destructive, ego-based behavior. As I witnessed Mike's healing, due to the insight he obtained by opening up and sharing his life's experiences, emotionally I was moved to bear witness to his soul's liberation. The clarity and understanding he gained motivated me to go deeper within myself, into the wombs that housed repetitive patterns of choices made from my ego. During my self-reflection, I recalled that when doing things for others, I would give my all as a friend. But if it was an intimate relationship, I wouldn't allow myself to get too emotionally involved with my girlfriend. I limited my love for her and didn't allow myself to love her the way that she should have been cherished. My excuses used were: I'm not getting stuck in a foreign country; I had my modeling and acting career to focus on. So, the love that I gave was conditional and limited (I recognize the choices that were made by me were similar to my father). Unfortunately, the consequence of those choices would result in my so-called friend's betrayal due to jealousy. But when the deception came from a girlfriend, I would just shrug it off and say my love was conditional because I knew how far I would emotionally allow myself to let go. When the friendships ended, I would be disappointed with myself because I had recognized the jealousy, but I chose to ignore it, thinking that it was too petty to confront them over it until they betrayed me.

As I self-reflected, I recognized that I was still putting myself in abandonment situations. Uncovering once again it's origins, I was still being affected by my parent's separation. The abandonment I felt from my father since the age of four was still emotional baggage I hadn't let go of. If it was not for my cousin Joseph's listening skills and wisdom, I may have never gained the insight that would help me to discern the illusion of my ego. I was disappointed to understand that I had not totally let go of the feeling of abandonment. As my cousin delicately guided me to the place where the pain existed, it was in that dark place that I found the answers to some of my emotional blocks. That night I went home, and while laying in bed, I reflected on the emotional discovery and spiritual healing that had taken place while hearing Mike's confession about his life experiences. If we could consciously take a step back and objectively observe our lives, would we ask ourselves what story we were presently writing by way of our own choices? If we were to become mindful of the many moments we rendered choices, would they likely be formulated by our emotions that support a false belief of self? The ego uses impressions that create emotions, and the energy from the emotions manifest into the physical. Examining the daily norms of many civilizations, we can clearly understand how it gets entangled in an ego state of mind. These untrue images and beliefs of who and what we believe ourselves to be continue to be distorted by the ego. This is causing generation after generation to continue acting out these inaccurate ideas of the soul. These falsehoods are continuing to be passed down for generations until the cycle is broken. *But how can it be halted?* I thought. *How am I going to recognize the ego in every choice I make?* I began to become anxious because of the perplexing process of such a daunting task. Suddenly, deep within my being, this calmness came over me because I knew that my compass to God could guide me out of the dark and back into the light of love. As I began to come down from the high of connecting with Spirit, I thought to myself, *But how do I reconnect to my inner child?* Unexpectedly, I knew in my soul that the answers were coming sooner rather than later, and I was ready to receive.

CHAPTER 6
THE INNER CHILD
BREAKING THE PATTERN

"The inner child is the Soul personified in its purest form within the physical body on the earth plane. And the inner child is the Soul personified in its highest and truest form within the light body that exist in other dimensions." —Ajana

Some days I would wake up in the morning, and after thanking God for life, I would notice from time to time the feeling of deep sadness. Sometimes the sorrow would hit me while sitting with friends in Madison Square Garden watching a New York Knicks basketball game. Or after one of my sexual conquests while coming down from the high of my ego feeling as if I was God's gift to the woman that lay next to me. Why did I still feel alone; I had just coalesced with someone, even if it was just for a moment in time? Occasionally I would try to justify my loneliness by convincing myself that it was because I was away from my family. Having resided in a foreign country cohabitating around an unfamiliar culture and language, this must be the reason why I felt alone? I would tell myself that would pass, all-the-while I continued entertaining myself by partying. I unconsciously attempted to mask the loneliness with alcohol and women. All the trappings of the physical world are designed to satisfy my ego. I tried to escape from the trappings of my ego by making an effort to avoid dealing with the stress of my modeling and acting career in my normal selfish ways, but instead I sometimes made a different choice by just going to the gym to release my pent up burdens. Some of my anxiety was brought about by the hopes of booking the next big gig as then I wouldn't have to worry about supporting myself, and I could live a financially independent lifestyle. But the deep sadness would come back. I didn't realize it then, but I was depressed at times. I would ask myself, *why am I so unhappy?* I was living abroad, my face was shown at home, while simultaneously being seen on television and magazines in different countries. I was around beautiful women and connecting with people from different parts of the world. There are some Americans who have never left the United States but dream of doing what I was experiencing, so why would I from time to time feel so alone?

One morning while lying in my apartment in Cape Town, I was feeling this deep sadness again. I heard my phone beep, I picked it up and looked at it, and it was a text from my boy Mario, it read, *"Hey Bernard, is everything OK? I thank God for crossing paths with you and us becoming friends. For when you were born, all of the universes and angels celebrated because of your existence. Be happy, I am grateful to have you as a friend."* I thought to myself, as I stared at my cell phone, *How did he know?* Because this text message came at the time when I was feeling down and needed to be uplifted. I wasn't aware at that moment, but God had heard my questions and prayers. This was the beginning of a number of intense spiritual healings of my mind, body and soul. Treatments that would allow me to reconnect to the dormant soul within myself. This reconnection would allow me to remember who I was and why Spirit created this specific existence for me to experience. Part of the pilgrimage was to reconnect me with my inner child self, 'My Compass to God'. I became aware that I wasn't going to take the journey alone; I felt that this was the beginning of a deep spiritual connection and brotherhood between Mario and me.

It was a hot summer's day in Cape Town. Mario and I were sitting on my balcony and I heard something different in his voice. It was stronger, even though he naturally had a deep voice, but there was something unusual about the tone of his voice that day. It sounded very wise and enthusiastic for some strange reason (later I would find out why). I felt deeply this elevated vibration around us, but I wasn't sure why. The sound of his voice had a wisdom that was coming far beyond our existence. Mario had an interesting life story; he came from a family of Ambassadors from Angola. His father and his mother's father represented their country in South Africa, he spoke five different languages, practiced three different martial arts, and he was spiritually gifted. At times we would have primitive conversations about what females we conquered; those who we loved or didn't allow ourselves to love. But the majority of our conversations were spiritual; with each discussion we would go spiritually deeper than the previous one.

On this day we began to converse. As I was about to get up to get something to drink, Mario asked assertively, "Where are you going, we have work to do?"

I responded sarcastically, "I'm going to get something to drink in my apartment—the last I checked, I paid rent monthly here."

As I walked away, I kept repeating it in my mind, that he had just asserted, "we have work to do." *That was an unusual thing to say,* I thought. But there was something about what he said that resonated within my being. I came back and sat down and heard Mario say in this strong powerful voice of wisdom, "Your godmother doesn't have much time left on this earth. When your mother passed away, your godmother took over the role of mother. Your mother raised you in God's light, and it was your godmother's role to take you higher spiritually from where your mother left off. She loves you as if you are her own, considering that she didn't have any children, but you are her child. Unfortunately, Bernard, she doesn't have much time left in this world."

I felt this deep sadness and pain within my heart because I couldn't imagine myself living without her. In my heart it was hurting so bad that in my thoughts I silently I asked, *God, am I going to lose another mother again?* I couldn't bear losing her. I wondered how Mario knew about my godmother, who just so happened to have the same name as my mother, Ann? Suddenly I felt overwhelmed with emotions, so much so that I wanted to weep, but I held it in because my ego-self wasn't going to show my emotions in front of him. While staring at me, Mario said, "Let it come out, you've held so many emotions in for so long." But I couldn't; I wouldn't cry, so I held it in. He casually stood up and walked towards me while ever so gently tapping me in the center of my chest near my heart. Suddenly, I was overcome with a flood of emotional sensations; the Levy's unconsciously built around my heart were broken and were now open for years of pent up emotions to spill out of me like never before. In what felt like the first time in allowing myself to feel, the emotions were so overwhelming that I broke down and sobbed a tsunami of tears.

I stood up and walked from the balcony into my kitchen because I did not want Mario to see me crying. I wailed a monsoon of tears like a child coming out of its mother's womb. I finally let go of all the pain that I had held inside for so long. Mario hugged me, and he started shedding a few tears of his own. At that moment I started reliving my mother's death, and the crossing over of my grandfather—two of the most important family members I was closest to. I cried out, "God! How can you take the only two women who truly loved me unconditionally, I'm going to really be alone in the world!"

As I gained control of my feelings, the process of releasing my emotions had healed a part of me that had been deeply wounded and suppressed within my heart for so many years. This was one of many healings that I would experience with Mario along my spiritual passage into the remembrance of who I truly was.

Unexpectedly again I heard this voice of Mario, ever so gently, however direct and powerful, say, "In order for you to reconnect with your inner child, you have to clear all of this stuff up here," pointing to my brain by tapping on the right side of my temple. He continued, "In order to get to here [pointing to my heart]. We have work to do—are you willing to do the work necessary in order to reconnect with your true self?

I answered, "Yes!"

Mario smiled, and the voice that was different from Mario said, "I am the inner child of Mario, his true self, his compass to God." He continued, "God must have heard my prayers because I always knew that I existed. I was told by the purest part of himself." Mario prayed to God for answers to this life, and when Mario prays, it's answered. "He prayed to God for you to reconnect to your inner child because he felt your pain."

In order to hear God, you have to listen in between the silence as that's where you can heed to the words of the divine. For that to happen, you have to clear your mind of negative thoughts. The ego uses thoughts, and thoughts create emotions, and emotions evolve and manifest into the physical plane, presenting themself in numerous facets, such as illness, anger, depression, or sadness, all cultivated from feeling unloved. All of the negative untruths that our ego would have us believe about ourselves, but our inner child understands that all of these lies are exactly what they reveal themselves to be. I proclaimed that I was not only going to get rid of my ego, but I would be permanently free of it.

Mario's inner child spoke and said, "Don't try to eradicate the ego—if it was not for the ego, you wouldn't know who you truly are. So, when you're having negative thoughts of lacking or feeling not good enough, now you are going to remember that you are not these adverse thoughts. But you are and always shall be a perfect, whole and complete being, the only way God created you to be. If you need to be reminded of who you truly are, observe a child. Children have the purest love—their souls are so pure until they are tainted by outside influences. They are impacted by their parents imposing their will upon them and so many societal judgments being placed upon them. Nevertheless, only the inner child can reconnect you with your inner child. Another way to declare that would be that only God's pure love can reconnect God's pure love with itself, not the ego."

We started doing some spiritual work within myself by exploring some intense areas of my being. I entered doorways that took me to the core of the problems that were governed by the ego. For the next twenty-eight days, Mario and I stayed within the compounds of my apartment working on clearing our minds of negative thoughts. We accomplished this task by constantly attacking my ego on a daily basis. The only time we ventured out of my Cape Town apartment was to get food. Some days, all the spiritual work that we were doing became so intense that we would force ourselves to go catch the last bit of sun before it set, or to behold a glimpse of the full moon. I was told by Mario's compass to God, my teacher, that from time to time that we should take breaks and go for walks to see God's creation. As I looked up at the constellations with Mario's true self, my instructor reminded me that what we were admiring were gifts from God for us to cherish because he was pleased with our progress. After almost a month being pushed by his inner child who continuously provoked my ego daily, I soon discovered that it didn't take long before my ego wanted to kill him many times over! Fortunately, I finally emerged victoriously different; I had reconnected with my inner child, the purest loving energy of the Divine, my inner child true self who I always was and forever shall be. I was oblivious that I was under the influence of my ego, resulting in me believing that I was who it wanted me to be. It influenced me to continue to unconsciously make choices that kept me caught up in the many false illusions of the ego. Now I see through the illusion, my inner child self-revealed the truth to me and set me free. Now I am aware of who I truly am, an extension of God's loving consciousness.

Our inner child selves are fearless. Once we nurture ourselves back to our true existence and become one with the purest part of us, we are able to tap into a power that knows no limits to create a phenomenal life with purpose. We gain a deeper understanding because our true selves remember that it is an extension of God. It knows that this omnipresent being is the source of its true existence. Before being born into this physical dimension, it's shown its true purpose. Knowing that it came onto this earth plane to do God's will. The purpose of a spiritual mission is to obtain spiritual growth while being in the services of the Divine. Fulfilling its purpose by creating a life that assists lost souls in finding their way back to the light. Existing as a lantern that illuminates the love of the Creator. Reminding souls to remember who they are by the awakening of their dormant soul.

Once this powerful, loving, spiritual part of you is awakened, it has the opportunity to experience a life filled with unlimited possibilities. We can live a life with awareness by staying connected to our compass to God. Our inner child enlightens us to make higher-level conscious choices that's Shepard by God. Only then do we begin to live a more meaningful life with purpose. As we continue to walk as our true selves, we will always be connected to our greatest potential. But in order to fulfill our life's purpose, we have to overcome many blocks that are created by making lower-level choices from our ego. Furthermore, the consequences of those choices cause us to live a life opposite of that of our true selves. The inner child does not dwell in the past, future, or within negative thoughts, which is the playground of the ego. It always remains in the present, and every thought, word, and deed is grounded in love. The essence of love is what fuels the inner child, motivating it to fulfill its destiny. It knows that it has a higher calling to create a world of joy, love, and peace by being its brother's keeper. It desires to create a better world—a utopian society only governed by the laws of love, creating a heaven on earth by fulfilling the will of God.

My mom in her younger years (1960's) Socializing in New York.

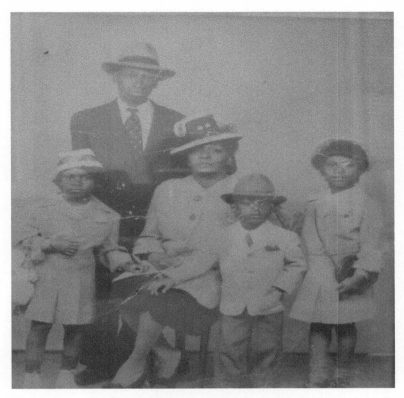

My father at age 15 (at the top left) with three of his siblings. Aunt Annie (center), his mother's sister took them in after his mother's death.

My father (on the right) on his wedding day with his first wife (far left)

My father in his early 20s with his first wife.

My Mom in the early '70s

Grand Mother Chaney, my Mom's mother

My parents last time together, at my brother Anthony and I high school graduation

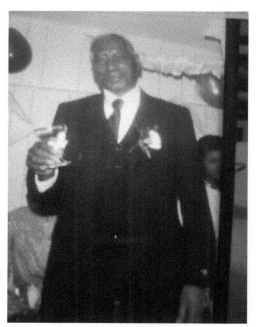

My father's third wedding

CHAPTER 7
LIVING WITH AWARENESS

"In order to know who you are, you have to know who you're not."—
Conversations with God

Living with awareness is being able to live in the present moment being mindful of what you're creating by way of your thoughts and emotions. While acting out our beliefs in the present moment, we should ask ourselves if we know if the impressions we're creating are emanating from a negative vibration or positive, calling into question whether the reflection will align us with Spirit, giving us access to the ability to manifest whatever we yearn for in accordance with God's will. By not dwelling in the past or future but simply existing as our true selves in the now, it will keep us connected to positive vibrations that will align us to infinite possibilities. However, in order to continue creating at a higher vibration, we must continuously observe who we are at that present moment by asking, is it our true selves or the ego? When I was reconnecting with my inner child-self, I had to go into the dark rooms that didn't house love to clear out the negative impressions of trauma that I harbored within.

Determined to overcome my burdens, I had to assault my ego by penetrating deep into the realms of my negative beliefs. I was hoping to uncover the cause that was creating anger and pain. As I self-reflected, I got closer to the inception of my temporary insanity that was triggered at times by my emotions. Suddenly, I had an epiphany! In order for healing to take place, I had to examine with perception what was triggering my emotions.

I knew one way to do this would be to use the writing exercise I was taught during the reconnection to my inner child. The way to use this exercise is you first must think of an emotionally negative experience you had, maybe in childhood or from a present-day experience that really hurt you or made you angry. For example, if you called your girlfriend to share an idea with her and she told you that she was breaking up with you because she needed someone to better support her financially, and all you had at that moment was nothing but a dream, then you find out that she's dating your best friend. Hearing her tell you this would not only be a devastating surprise, but a heartbreaker. The way to use the writing exercise is to think of a painful or furious occurrence to pull from; it could be a resent or past ordeal. Recall the incident as if it was happening in the present moment. While reliving the experience, allow the sensations from the pain and anger to reemerge. Use all of that emotional energy and write down how you feel about the ordeal with that person. Allow the anger to rise up in you, documenting all of your negative thoughts and feelings in its entirety. Don't be afraid of expressing on paper some of your dark emotions. Continue to jot down what you may want to do or say to that person as if they were standing in front of you. List all of the unfavorable thoughts you may have about them, permitting the dark recollections to continue to emerge, propelling you deeper into unloving vibrations. By continuously having depressing thoughts and anger outbursts, this should be the motivation for you to want to resume the exercise. Remember to burn all of the pages while saying a prayer, or repeat a positive statement about releasing your negative thoughts after each writing session. Keep repeating this exercise until the destructive thinking starts to subside, slowly freeing your mind from self-defeating beliefs. Soon what will happen is that you should start to experience gaps in your thoughts, and in that space is where you will hear your true self. When you're in this space, your inner child self will be your compass, guiding you back to the light of truth. Be still and listen in-between the silence, that's where you will hear God, the highest truth, guiding us out of the darkness, back to the source of our existence.

Once I was reconnected with my inner child, I started living life with more awareness. Whenever my ego tried to present itself as a false sense of me, by way of my thoughts, words, or actions keeping me preoccupied with thoughts from the past, I would evade those thoughts by bringing myself back into the present moment by asking myself, *Who's impressions are these? Are they of my true self, or my ego?* Were my thoughts about something that happened in the past or something I hoped to achieve in the future? If the answer to those questions was yes, then I was certain that it was my ego. The way I snapped out of receiving impressions from my ego was effortlessly done. I would just change my thoughts once I'd become aware that they were negative; I easily changed them to optimistic thoughts, being mindful of how the thoughts were making me feel at that time. Our inner child is always existing in the present moment because the power of creation is always in the present, not the past. The present moment is where the future is conceived. The ego shows up in various forms, so I wondered how I would know when I'm acting out in my ego and not as my true self? I recalled the twenty-eight days I attacked my ego with the writing exercise. By using the exercise daily, it helped me to reconnect to my true self. Mario's ego persistently triggered mine, and each time I responded back he would ask me who was speaking. "Is it your true self, or is it your ego speaking?"

Another way of knowing I wasn't being my true self was by observing my actions with whomever I crossed paths with. I would observe my thoughts and emotions after gaging how I left them. Was it a positive exchange or a negative one? If we parted and it was a positive exchange, then I knew I was walking as my true self. If it was the opposite experience, then I knew I was walking as my ego. By observing my daily actions and discerning the outcome of my choices. I slowly began to differentiate from my ego and my inner child. Practicing this enabled me to understand where I was formulating my choices from and whether the thoughts were of a higher oscillation or lower.

Being aware of who we're not helps us to develop a clear picture of our true selves. The ego uses thoughts, thoughts create emotions, and emotions convince us to believe that we're whatever feelings we believe ourselves to be. Sure enough, it manifests, and we become what we perceived in our psyches. The impressions of the ego can be very persuasive; it bombards our minds with negative thoughts, repeatedly formulating ideas of not being good actions enough, thoughts that keep us caught up in the mirage of the world. Mankind becomes so preoccupied with the daily dramas on the job and within our family that it coerces us into a negative energy flow. We then began to only recognize the dysfunctions in the world, and by doing this, it continues to defend our belief in the fallacy within an egotistical civilization. This discourages souls from remembering who they truly are until we decide not to continue living as dormant souls, allowing ourselves to be distracted by our emotions.

As I continued to do the spiritual soul work, the more it assisted in getting rid of the falsehoods of my ego. When I occasionally fell back into my old ways by making the same lower vibrational choices, I began to experience the consequence of those choices. I became aware of my discretions because I began to grow tired of the outcome of my choices; they didn't manifest the best experiences for me. I got so tired of running in a circle until I made a conscious decision to do something about it.

One day I was working out with this model from my agency, Francois. I had been practicing a yoga breathing exercise for a couple of years and had previously suggested to Francois to take The Art of Living Happiness course. I had recommended it to him for a number of reasons, but mainly because he was suffering from anxiety attacks, and at the time he was smoking thirty joints a day. A few months had passed since he had taken the course with amazing results. He no longer smoked weed or cigarettes, and his days of suffering from anxiety attacks had ended, but the most profound healings were more internal. I had been practicing The Art of Living doing the Kriya exercise (breathing, yoga, meditation) for about two years, but I was a little disappointed that I wasn't as flexible as I thought I should be. I coaxed Francois into doing a power yoga workout with me, well aware and envious of his nimble capabilities considering his size. I previously had observed him during an instructed yoga class we had taken. So, my ego was determined to do as well as he did by tolerating the discomfort and completing the yoga postures, enduring till the end of the session.

Before we began, I made sure to stretch well because I didn't want to struggle to transition from one yoga stance into the next. As I shifted from the downward-facing dog position back down onto my knees, my arms extended straight in front of me while resting my buttocks on the back of my legs, unexpectedly, something remarkable began to happen while I was in the child's pose (a position every infant is in while developing in its mother's womb). I noticed that I wasn't shifting out of the stance. In my mind's eye, I abruptly saw a vision of my father, then I saw a vision of my mother who happened to be glowing, dressed in all white. My father had passed away two years prior, so I wasn't reflecting on his life or our dysfunctional relationship at all. Suddenly at that moment, this rage began to build in my heart, and in my mind's eye, I was looking directly at my father. Suddenly, in that space and time, we both existed within the same realm. I began yelling and pounding my fist on the floor as tears continuously erupted from the depths of my heart. Simultaneously I directed a bunch of profanities towards him; I wanted him to feel all the pain and anger I had carried for so long all bottled up inside. He deserved to know the trauma inflicted upon me as a child. As the burst dame of tears continued to flow out of me, I even had a few choice words for my mother. It was a surreal moment that felt as if I was having an out-of-body experience.

Suddenly my deceased parents disappeared from my mind's eye as quickly as they entered. I slowly began to emerge from this unusual circumstance; I began placing my hands individually on the top of my head, forehead, throat, heart, and stomach area, breathing in and out at each placement. I was feeling a little bewildered about what I had just experienced. Not quite understanding what had just transpired. I was stunned to hear Francois tell me that I was in the child's pose for about an hour. That was astonishing to me because it felt as if it wasn't long at all. I thought it couldn't have been any longer than fifteen minutes.

He asked, "Bernard, when you were touching certain areas of your body and breathing, who taught you how to do that?" I explained that no one had, I just intrinsically moved my hands to those areas and placed them there.

Francois was amazed, he asked again, "Are you sure you haven't seen me doing that?"

"Didn't I say no, why?"

He explained, "Because I'm a Reiki healer, and those are the areas of our chakras where we can be healed from."

As I analyzed the life-changing experience I had endured, I came to understand that I had never totally forgiven my father, though I believed I had done so. My true self was aware of the blocks that existed in my heart due to the unresolved dysfunctional relationship with my father. The unforgiven issues that were hidden in the dark niches of my heart needed to be uncovered in order to bring about healing. My liberation from the emotional bondage unbeknownst to me that I was being held captive. I was under the impression that I had forgiven my father, but I was mistaken. I was amazed to discover that the ordeal I had just experienced helped clear the way for a deeper connection with God.

I came to understand that the more profound the healing, the greater the awareness. I had gained an in-depth understanding of the multiple layers of the ego. Having obtained clarity about who I wasn't, I became encouraged to start making higher vibrational choices as my true self. If we desire to recognize the true essence of our inner child, tap into that child-like energy. Always centered in and beaming out the purest unconditional love of Spirit. Connection with Spirit comes effortlessly when we recall that we are aspects of God while enduring life in the physical plane. Retaining awareness of this helps us to make higher vibrational choices that personify a magnificent life for us to experience and share with others.

CHAPTER 8
SEEING THROUGH THE ILLUSION

"Bless each person who comes into your life and brings you pain... for who stands before you is your greatest teacher."—Conversation with God

We are co-creators living a life of endless manifestations. Our life lessons create possibilities for enormous conscious awakenings pointing us towards our true existence. I like to describe them as shakes from our soul. Whether we are conscious of it or not, our soul presents life predicaments to us, but what's incorporated in those dilemmas exist a summation of all our past choices. However, the fortunes of our intentions depends on how extremely influenced we were by our parent's conditioning, be it positive or negative. My mom wasn't a good manager of money; instead of her paying off one bill, she would divide the money and pay a little bit on each bill. This would keep her in debt because she was always behind. As I grew into manhood, I began to notice some blocks passed on to my siblings and me, and one of those issues was the fear of lacking. Even though today most of us are making a nice enough income, taking overseas trips, purchasing properties, and making investments, having obtained comfortably a materialistic lifestyle that my mother could only dream of having. Instead, her dreams would be placed on hold because of the selfless sacrifices she would make for her children's future. My mom's differed dreams enabled us to be able to acquire our ambitions of living a life better than the one she had to endure. Yet despite our successes, my siblings and I still carried the fear of not having enough.

Deciding to take some time to be silent solely to self reflect on my life, I concluded that my money supervision wasn't much different than my mothers. Within my psyche, I did have the fear of lacking. When I received money, I felt that I wouldn't have enough left after paying my debts, so I partially paid them. I may not have been conscious of it, but I lived with the fear of lacking. Yet my lifestyle may have displayed an image contrary to that because of my travels around the world. Ultimately, my unsuspecting fear of scarcity would become my truth when I sometimes arrived in a country with a limited amount of money. I would be praying that I would finally book that big modeling campaign or film role, hoping that God would be kind because I took a chance and flew there by faith. Surely that alone should prove that I truly trust him.

At the beginning of my modeling career, I had flown from Paris to Milan just two months prior, and I was residing in a country that had cultural pride, especially in their Italian cuisine and fashion. One evening, I logged into my journal to write down my daily reflections, beginning with thanking God for the gift of life, a roof over my head, and food to eat. With the same stroke of my pen, I easily contradicted my gratitude for my blessings by triggering an anxiety attack with feeling a sense of deficiency. My reflections were, *I'm down to my last $65 and rent is due, I'm sure something will come through?* Instead of having faith, I acted out in fear. I got the idea to call my sister, Sharon, to ask her for financial assistance. I speculated to myself that the family must be excited about my travels having decided to pursue my dreams, so she will help. I dialed her number and when she answered, I shared with her the adventures of my travels and the hopes and dreams I manipulated my thoughts to believe. That I would soon book big modeling or acting gigs, but I needed to borrow some money from her for rent. Her response was, "Look, you chose this life, so now you are going to have to make it happen or come home."

Her words rung in my ears and pierced my heart. I knew she was speaking sensibly, but that wasn't the response I'd imagined in my mind that I would hear. I dreamt that I would hear her telling me how proud she was of me and that she would send me whatever I need, but I was delusional to believe that would happen. As the shock wore off and my ego began to kick in, I suddenly became upset. When I was on the phone, I didn't tell her how I truly felt, instead I thanked her and expressed that something will come through, that I'll book a big job. I told her that I loved her and hung up the phone. After ending the phone call, I felt a little hurt. I thought to myself, *How could my family not want to assist me? I'm living abroad in a foreign country, pursuing my dreams, and I couldn't get any help; she has the money.*

In hindsight, that lesson Sharon unknowingly taught me coerced me to take a sincere psychological look at myself to understand why I wasn't financially succeeding and affording me the ability to remain in Milan until I accomplish my endeavors. I recognized that there was no need for me to get upset with her when she only spoke her truth, facts that exposed the reality that I needed to heed. Well, needless to say, I lived in Milan for a year and booked jobs that made me more than enough capital to continue pursuing my dreams. Unfortunately, it wasn't easy undoing the mental conditioning of lacking; it would take me some time before I could cease the repetitive mistakes of acting out of fear instead of faith.

As I intensified my self-reflection, the more I discovered the little demons I possessed that I wasn't aware of, such as, social drinking, slumbering with any girl that came along (I was close to my Grandfather since childhood, and I'd heard that throughout his marriage he committed many adulterous acts, repeating what his father had done), and repeating the cycle of infidelities in my relationships. The only females I did commit to were the ones that I felt I could count on, and they were just a few. My excuses were, 'I'm focusing on my career' or ' I can't get too serious because I'm not having any children living abroad'. It wasn't clear to me at that moment, but the sins of my father were emotionally affecting my ability to commit. When I did get into a relationship, I would forgo my emotions because I felt that she wasn't the one. What caused me to wake up and face my demons was this girl I knew in New York. We met through a friend of mine; she was the sister of his best friend, and Amy was in her last semester of college. She was tall with big beautiful brown eyes, a nice body, and face that could rival Naomi Campbell. Amy left New York soon after graduating to go overseas to perform with a dance troupe in Europe. Two years later she returned and began dancing on Broadway. There were many reasons why I was attracted to Amy. She was very attractive, confident, and highly intelligent, and she had evolved into a successful professional artist. Some time had passed and we both had matured due to the many adventures and experiences while pursuing our dreams. As I stared into her beautiful eyes, I thought about how life had been kind to her because she looked amazing as I saw light gleaming from her soul.

At this stage in my life I was living fully in my ego—my career was growing, and my ego was sustained by the trappings of the entertainment industry. In the past I didn't treat some women well. Though I had a lot of love and respect for them, what sustained me from losing total respect was the love I had for my mother. Still, I didn't fully permit myself to emotionally let go, allowing myself to fully love them the way that they should have been adored. My insincerity got me so caught up in the illusion of life, how could I put a limit on expressing the love that God generously gives to us? To be honest, I didn't know who I was, but I would soon unsuspectingly have a rude awakening to that awareness. Unfortunately, during that time, I had no understanding of my ego. I believed that was who I truly was. Until my heart confirmed the feelings I felt for this professional dancer were true. For the first time, it gave me the courage to emotionally let go. Unfortunately, I reaped what I had sowed. I experienced all of the not-so-great things that I had done to a woman. My karma had been served, and I don't believe she was ever aware that she played a big part in my soul's emotional transformation. My ego was crushed; I tried to act as if it didn't bother me as I had easily done so many times with other women, but on this day, I couldn't hide it because my heart had spoken loud and clear. This painful experience brought attention to my misbehaviors. It revealed all of the wrongdoings I had inflicted upon those women; I may have thought of it as being nothing major because I believed that that was just how men were (what did I truly know about being a man? I learned on my own by not having a father figure mentoring me most of my life). I wasn't mentally or emotionally attentive to the pain my actions produced in others. Once again, my soul brought forth another life lesson that reminded me of who I truly was, which was the opposite of the pain that I had inflicted on others. The clarity I obtained from that experience assisted in the emergence of a deeper connection with my true self by showing me my repetitive patterns and the consequences of my actions. I had to feel the pain I administered in my past relationships. I felt a desire to explore deeper within my existence to penetrate the illusion of my ego, prompting me of a more powerful loving presence within.

To know who I was, I had to know who I was not. One day I had a flashback to when I was a teenager. I recalled my mother saying to me once that I was "just like my father." At that stage in my life, I thought that was the most dreadful thing she could ever say to me because I didn't believe that I was anything like my father. Our personalities clashed a lot, and as I matured the more, I judged and related his inadequacies to his personality. I didn't enjoy my visits with my father because I'd likely have to work and listen to him give me a lecture about life. Listening to my father speak about my existence was strange considering that he wasn't in my life much as a child. His favorite topics of conversation were women, education, and being a leader. During one of my visits, while helping him paint (more like working for his financial contribution), I reached into my bag and pulled out a beer. As I opened it, his reaction was one of disbelief because it was his first time witnessing his son drink alcohol, and he was shocked! I knew this because I'd never seen my father's eyes open so wide—he looked as if he had seen a ghost.

As he quickly regained his composure and calmly said to me "Since when have you been able to drink?"

I elucidated my explanation with, "Since I became old enough to drink, I'm twenty-one!"

He paused, perhaps thinking for a moment, and said, "That must be your mothers doing."

I felt as if I had won a small battle ,and that victory never felt so good. My father didn't drink; the only thing he indulged in was smoking Lucky Strikes cigarettes, drinking tea, and having an intellectual conversation that always turned into a debate. Depending on whether you were either the teacher or the student, you either taught or learned something new, and most of the time my father was the teacher. My pops had a gift; while in a discussion he could find the weakness in others, exposing it by provoking their emotions. When he would obtain this small victory, he would sit back and laugh as he enjoyed his small conquest.

I had a young and defiant temperament with my father, and II was convinced that I wasn't listening to anything he had to say. I would let it go in one ear and out of the other, or so I thought. I wouldn't realize it until years later that it had permeated my mind and soul. I came to appreciate over the years that he had shared with us his wisdom. There's a saying that 'time makes a man wiser'. I understood that expression when I had to heal from one of the most traumatic experiences of my young life—the death of my mother. That ordeal caused my search for a deeper understanding of the purpose of life, creating many questions for God, and the answers to those questions propelled me closer to Spirit. Did I seek an explanation from him because I always wondered why my father never fully committed to my mother? What stopped him from deeply loving her and not taking that step towards marriage? These questions steered me toward wanting to know more about the life of the man who held the mysteries to the other strands of my DNA.

CHAPTER 9
CONSCIOUSLY MANIFESTING THE POWER OF THOUGHT WORD AND DEEDS

The spiritual gifts God has assigned to us are many, but some gifts are only allotted to a select few. One of these blessings that are bestowed to us all but taken for granted by most souls is manifestation. God's light exists in all of his creations, and the soul is just an extension of God's light giving birth to a physical experience. Unfortunately, most of what we are manifesting and experiencing is done unconsciously. What is given at birth is the free will to choose, but our discretions are made from either our higher selves (love) or lower (ego). If we observe today's world, the majority of mankind's choices couldn't possibly be made from a loving state of mind.

We are constantly making choices, even when we don't choose, we've made one. Once a choice is made, it's sent out into the universe, and it has no choice but to bring forth what we have chosen, delivering the repercussions of those choices. Hindus call it 'Karma', in Christianity it's 'you sow what you reap'. The Buddhists call it 'cause and effect', all meaning the same and delivering equivalent results. So, when the repercussions of our choices return back to the home of its inception, the experiences may turn out to be unpleasant ones; we may cry out, "Why has God allowed this bad luck, disappointment, and pain to happen to me?"

One of our most common excuses we use is the Devil. For instance, 'the Devil made me drink which caused me to sleep with that married woman, resulting in my wife finding out about the affair, and now she wants a divorce'. But the truth is, you've experienced unhappiness because of the problems in your marriage. But the difficulties emerged from past choices that were manifested from thoughts of a lower vibration.

When we become aware of our choices, we begin to notice which part of ourselves we are choosing to create from. Once we began to understand that our intentions open a doorway, that allows entrance into the beginning of an enormous awakening. A knowing that is achieved by choosing to live in the present moment. The most important path to manifesting your heart's desires and dreams because there is no time in God expanse. Unexpectedly, we begin to take responsibility for our actions, desiring a better outcome from our previous choices because the old ways of choosing were no longer adequate. Change comes quickly when decisions are habitually made from a higher consciousness. By tapping into a different aspect of our self, our inner child, the part of us that's perfect, whole, and complete. This loving, caring part of us will guide us back to the source of our purest higher selves. Then, and only then, can we live and create as Christ did. From a place of peace and pure love. For the desire for us to choose to manifest at this high level, we must constantly ask ourselves, *From what place are my thoughts manifesting from? Is it from the emotional side of the Ego, or is it from my true self?*

We should make time within our daily lives to sit in silence twice a day, doing nothing but taking slow deep breaths, clearing our thoughts until we connect to our true selves. By committing to do our spiritual practice and proclaiming positive affirmations daily, it raises our vibrations, making us susceptible to connect to the Source of our existence. With God's guidance, it helps us to engage with that deeper part of our existence. We begin to silence the negative thoughts that create feelings of doubt, anger, self-judgment, and fear. These emotions will continue to exist as lead actors on the stage in our minds, positioning the ego as the director of this repetitive production that's continuously playing out in our psyche until we put an end to what was created. The shift is achieved in silence, breaking the constant negative daily drama in our lives. If we don't go within to truly understand our purpose existing on this planet, we are doomed to fail if we continue to believe the false impressions of the ego's selfish manipulations of our thoughts. It is just a mental distraction that keeps us from realizing our true inner power. An awakening occurs when we begin to hear in-between the silence the guidance of the highest truth, once again reminding us of how divine we are.

The more I uncovered about who I truly was, the deeper I became my true self. I recall being told that though we will have to answer for our previous discretions made, we are able to change our prior intentions and that of our forefathers by making different choices that will create a different future. Nevertheless, who we truly are is an extension of the highest truth, who happened to have never left us alone, but always has and forever shall be with us. After all, as we experience this life as a human, who is the one who gave us free will? I recall while being in my quite space that God gave us the tools (spiritual gifts) to utilize while on our life journeys. We have been sent many teachers to remind us that we have the power to consciously create, manifesting a life that brings heaven on earth. An indication that we have the authority to exemplify a life of love over and over again by thoughts, words, and deeds. These impressions manifested into the physical by the power of the tongue. Creating a much stronger vibration, easily bringing our desires into our existence much quicker. When these steps are used to create from a level of love while in the present moment of now, the God force within gives us the ability to effortlessly do miraculous things. Connecting to this power is how we can start to dispose of the sins of our parents by undoing and consciously manifesting a more perfect, whole, and complete life of wonder through healing.

By using the power of thoughts and speaking our intentions, we can heal and create a much healthier body. Just by sitting quietly and breathing into that perfect image of what it is you want to have, knowing that it is so. See it as if you are living that desire in that present moment. Having a clear thought about what it is you want to have, injecting loving emotions of gratitude and release it out to God. If practiced daily while you're in your quiet space or throughout the day, constantly daydreaming about your ambitions, you will start to see your destiny unfold. Remember to always give gratitude and know that it is done.

One day I walked into my modeling agency in South Africa to speak with the owner about finding better accommodation for me. The housing that was previously shown was so terrible that I walked in, didn't like what I saw, turned around and walked out. As I continued to describe the conditions of the housing I was shown, my agent, Neal, began to laugh and told me that he would see what he could do. I was angry because I normally find my own accommodation, but me depending on him to find housing wasn't a major concerned of his. After sleeping on a friend's couch for three days, I decided to go visit my acting agents. As I entered the office and said my hello's to the everyone, I sat down in front of my agent's desk and asked if she happened to know of someone renting accommodation because my model agency seems to be of no help. Susie lifted up her head with a big smile as she leaned forward towards me with her hands folded on top of her desk and said, "Bernard, I think Emma has a place for you, speak to her."

After speaking to Emma, she said, "Here," and handed me a set of keys. "It's my girlfriend's place, go take a look at it, I'm sure you will like it." I left the agency not believing how things were so easily aligning up for me, I didn't expect much but I hoped that I would like it.

When I arrived, I turned the keys to unlock the front door. When I entered the apartment, I was pleased with what I saw; the kitchen and dining room both blended into the living room space. I had forgotten that Emma informed me that the apartment was left furnished upon awaiting on her girlfriends return. The furnishing was modern with beige wood floors and two large, picturesque windows. As I looked around, I was more than pleased with what I had seen, but I couldn't see the bedrooms. To my astonishment, I was surprised to see a staircase because I didn't recall Emma telling me that there was a second floor. With each step I took, I ascended up to the second floor that revealed two bedrooms and a full bathroom; I was stunned! I was so surprised that I didn't remember how I got from the second floor, and I ended up downstairs sitting on the couch.

I couldn't stop giving thanks and wondering how I was granted this blessing. Until I heard Spirit say, "But you manifested this—you asked for this, you wrote it down." To my surprise, I remembered that I had written down my heart's desires and kept the letter in my Bible. I quickly ran upstairs to retrieve the letter that I hadn't looked at since I had last written it. As I read the list, I was astonished to see that I had received what I had asked for, and more! I was now living a half block from the sea on a dual floor, two-bedroom, and a bath and a half apartment. I was so humbled and grateful that I asked Spirit if I consciously manifested this? The reply I got was "yes." Do we have the actual power of creation to bring what we ask for into existence? The answer is yes, we are creating all the time, whether we're aware of it or not. But even though I knew this to be true, I still wasn't confident with me intentionally manifesting with awareness. I still needed more confirmations, and I would soon be given that assurance.

I had always wanted to travel to India to experience one of the oldest living cultures. One of my many longings was to lay eyes on the magnificent Taj Mahal. So, I created a vision board, placing on it some of my ambitions I wished to fulfill, visualizing them throughout the day and frequently giving gratitude. Until one day, my dreams became a reality. As I stood in front of this beautiful creation, questioning if what I was seeing was truly the Taj Mahal? I thought to myself, *I need proof that it is before I wake up and all of this was just a dream.* So, I asked this Indian couple that was walking by if they would be so kind and take a picture of me. Here I was standing in front of one of the most magnificent monuments in the world. I thanked them for taking the photo then I took a look at the image they had taken. While glancing at it, I had the thought of my vision board. That was odd because I hadn't thought of it until now, and it was created six months ago. Suddenly it dawned on me, that my trip to India had manifested itself into the present moment without an effort. But doubt soon crept into my thoughts; I began to question if I had done so. I tried to remember if I had cut a picture from the magazine brochure with the word 'India' printed on it, or if the picture on the vision board was the Taj Mahal? I laughed out loud thinking about the possibility of it being true. I couldn't wait to get back to my Cape Town apartment to see what the answer would be. Unfortunately, the discovery of the truth would have to wait because in a few hours I was headed to the United Arab Emirates, destination: Dubai.

When my time in Dubai came to an end, I was finally able to catch a flight back to Cape Town. As I entered the door to my apartment, I dropped my bags and ran into my bedroom to take a look at my vision board. I stood there in disbelief, and suddenly I was overcome with joy because my eyes were not deceiving me. I was so excited because what I was seeing on my vision board was a picture of the Taj Mahal, not just a cover with the words printed, but both. The only difference between the photo of me that was taken in India and the cut out of the magazine cover that was posted on my board was that in the photograph, I was standing in front of the Taj Mahal! I laughed; I couldn't believe that I consciously manifested an amazing adventure—a trip to India.

I enjoy going on pilgrimages to different counties and exploring my adventurous side during my travels. I enjoyed going to exotic places, such as India. I traveled the country by train like a local having seen the old trains that hadn't changed much, like in the old films I saw. What also peaked my fascination with the fleet was the inception of them being built so many decades ago, and they we're still running. I traveled by train to so many different destinations, cities like Varanasi and Rishikesh existing for over four thousand years. I was told that Christ had visited there. So, I had to remind myself to take a picture of the interior of the sleep cars. Finally, an opportunity presented itself on my last day in India. While traveling from the South up to the Northwest of the country, it was either now or never because tomorrow morning I was continuing my journey to the United Arab Emirates. It was late in the evening in Mumbai as the train pulled into Victoria station. I was the last passenger left in my sleep car, so I quickly jumped out of my seat as the train was slowly pulling into the station. I finally had my chance to take a picture, so I stepped out of the carriage to observe the image I wanted to capture. Within the chambers there were two large windows, and in between the windows was a small mirror, below the mirror was a table where you could eat. I took out my camera and snapped a picture. When I got back to the hotel, I wanted to look at the images of my trip. Unexpectedly, I had the idea to zoom into the picture taken of the sleeping car and then into the small mirror. So I did just that. As I looked closely into the mirror in the photo, I could see the image of myself taking the picture of the sleep car reflecting back at me. As I looked even closer at the image of myself, I noticed that there were two white circles of light. One of the orbs floated in front of my right shoulder, and behind me above my left shoulder was another sphere of white light. I became so excited because in my heart I knew what they were; these celestial beings were always with me giving me guidance and protection. This gave me the confirmation I needed that Angels exist. At that very moment, while holding the image in my hand, I was overcome with the feelings of so much love and gratitude. I knew in my heart that God had once again shown me, with living examples, how I manifested those experiences in my life and more. I was reminded that we all possess the power to create extraordinary lives for ourselves, validating what I subconsciously knew deep within my heart: that we are never alone at any time during this human existence.

CHAPTER 10
WE ARE NOT ALONE

"If you want to go somewhere fast, go alone if you want to go somewhere far go together."—African proverb

One night I heard this voice; it was so clear and direct, giving me the answers that I sought. I was living in Paris, modeling, experiencing life fully in my ego. I was partying, enjoying the ladies, and sociably drinking, a lot! At that time when I heard the voice of God, I was living with this French girl who liked me. She was a nice girl who had been through a tragic experience that caused the loss of one parent. Her mother's death was caused by the hands of her life partner, the one who was supposed to protect her. There was an argument between them and the husband, who happened to be a police officer, ended the dispute with a gunshot that instantly killed her mother. So here I was, living with a girl that I didn't care about only because I needed a place to live. Having found free accommodation, or so I thought, I would end up having to spiritually and financially make restitution for the choices that I made. What bothered me the most was that it was going against the moral teachings of my mother.

I knew that I wasn't raised to conduct myself in that manner. Due to that choice, I believe that was the reason my modeling work (among other things) had started to slow down until it came to an unexpected halt. I would later learn a discourse from my soul that everything in life that's done with good intentions, and with God's approval, comes without any negative consequences. But I was living a lie by giving her false impressions of formulating a loving relationship with her. I would later find out that my little falsehoods weren't going to bring forth a positive outcome.

I tried multiple times to convince myself that living with her was a good thing because I was going to comfort her with the intent of hopefully helping her soul to heal. But in my heart, I knew that it wasn't true at all because this went against my morals. I knew in my heart that I didn't have the same feelings for her that she had for me. My sentiments came from the conveyance of physical pleasure. I had made a promise to myself that I would never live with a woman to be finically taken care of, I would always have my own. So, this living situation that I was caught up in went against all my principles and it was eating me up inside. After all, what kept me in line was the fact that I was my mother's son.

Suddenly, I had this flashback of when we were kids, and my mom was reiterating these principles into my sibling's and I psyches. She would say, "I'm not going to have a house full of babies due to my girls having them at an early age and unmarried. I will also not tolerate a house filled with lazy unmotivated men—you either work, study, or do both."

It's funny because years later as my siblings and I became adults, the prophecy came to fruition the way my mother wanted it. Those who had children didn't have many. My two eldest sisters had the most children; one has three, and the other has two sons. My other siblings each have one, besides my brother Anthony and I at the moment. I guess my mother wanted us to have a better life than she had; she sacrificed a lot just to give us the chance to fulfill our dreams. With her prayers and guidance, she hoped that we would make intelligent life choices. Her life confessions pointed us in the directed away from strife, instead of towards a path that warranted a much positive outcome if chosen. I have siblings with a Ph.D., double masters, computer science, business, and associates degrees, and a brother and sister who are entrepreneurs. I learned that you must be aware of what testimonies you speak into your children's intellect as words are powerful. Being raised by a single mom, I was taught to always be self-sufficient. I tried to convince myself that I wasn't breaking any spiritual rules because I just needed a place to stay, and that would keep me in a favorable stature with God.

So here I was, breaking my moral compass. I was living with a French girl that I didn't have feelings for, who happened to be not only be providing accommodation, but also feeding me because I was broke. One evening I entered the apartment and was pleased to find that I was alone. I needed to have some quiet time, a moment to reflect and clear my mind. I was unhappy and disheartened that I was in this situation; I couldn't understand how I allowed myself to get in this position (at that time I wasn't aware of the power of choice), I didn't have a clue. I plopped myself down onto the bed, and for a moment I was caught up in a trance. While staring at my feet, I began to come out of my stupor. I lowered my head and proceeded to take off my shoes. Letting out a sigh of pessimism, I fell back on the bed with my feet still touching the floor. As I laid on my back, staring up at the ceiling, I began to search my thoughts. I needed to analyze what I was experiencing in my life, and I desperately needed answers. So, I cried out to God, speaking in a forceful voice, and I started asking him questions. How did I get into this situation? I don't have feelings for this girl, but haven't I treated her with respect?

I was trying to bargain with God with the hope of getting approval for my actions. I also asked, "Why isn't my career going well?" The more questions I asked, the more frustrated I became. Unexpectedly, I fell into this deep sleep, yet I was cognizant of what was transpiring. While in this unconscious state, I saw nothing but darkness. It appeared as if I was glancing downward into a pit as dark as the night sky that was absent of the light of the moon and stars. Suddenly, I saw what appeared to resemble two stars spiraling downward. As I observed this, I heard a voice say, "I always told you my child that I would never leave you, sometimes one light has to fall for the other light to rise." As I heard the voice of God speaking to me, I saw one star began to spiral upward. Then it spoke again, this enormous voice of God repeating the name "Job! Job! Job!" When I woke up from what seemed to be the true reality, I kept repeating the name Job in my mind. Although I'd read the Bible many times before, I wasn't familiar with the story of Job, nor had I retained enough to be able to quote scriptures from memory. I decided to get my Bible out to look up what I repeatedly heard the voice exclaim so that I could read about the story of Job. After reading about Job's many difficulties and trials in his life, I thought to myself, *Wow! Why am I complaining about my situation?* The story of Job deeply resonated within my being. I was so humbled by the experience because I knew that I was spoken to by God. At that moment, an understanding came over me. It confirmed that he had always heard me call out to him during the difficult times in my life. The awareness that I gained was that we are never alone on this journey, for God is omnipresent.

In an instant, I knew that God had given me a Jewel. I was shown the difficulties in someone else's life that were far greater than what I was going through at that time. I was able to read how Job overcame his many obstacles, teaching me that trust and faith is a powerful mindset to have. That discourse forever changed my life. I recognized that to get out of my self-made situation, I had to trust the process. So, I went further into my existence to investigate why I was making these lower-level choices. At that moment, I made a conscious decision to manifest a change in my life. That decision brought me deeper into the inner journey of the self, a place unbeknownst to me that lead to the lives of my ancestors. Along this path, my ancestor's stories began to unravel. I discovered that womanizing, alcohol, and some abuse were prevalent throughout my grandparent's marriage, especially when my grandfather drank. I discover that some of these dysfunctions existed on both sides of my parent's families. As my investigation into the lives of the different generations within my lineage went on, a story started to unravel.

I noticed a pattern, not only within my family, but in the family of others. I noticed how we are all affected by the repercussions of our ancestor's choices. They imposed their opinions about life upon our vulnerable young minds, and in turn influenced our belief system, governing how we may believe life to be by having a negative or positive impact upon it. I discovered in God's divine plan, each of our families were chosen to experience this life together as a soul group. Just as a singular soul is experiencing itself (though not alone) to remember who it truly is. Soul groups (family) experience their life lessons collectively, hopefully overcoming them together. Benefiting from the blessing that are passed from one generation to the other, but so are their sins if not overcome. The challenge is discovering the individual soul work that needs to be done by withstanding the obstacles by learning the many life lessons as a family and those that are obtained externally. Each family leaves a blueprint of the tribe's history that's hidden, desiring to be uncovered. Hopefully to be used for the spiritual ascension, not only for their family, but by contributing to the awakening of humanity. I imagine that one-day humanity will realize that we are all one world family, joined together functioning from the place of love. I can only visualize how much different this world would be.

The more I pondered on God's words when he spoke to me, the more I struggled to discern why he told me that he would never leave me? Was it because at times I felt alone? I came to understand that not only has God time and time again sent us many teachers, but numerous others are assisting us? Once I became aware of these beings, I began to appreciate that we all have spirit guides, protectors, and Guardian Angels. Whatever title we may want to label them, they all serve one purpose, and that's to do God's will. They are always with us, waiting for us to call upon God, asking him for assistance and protection. The Angels are the ones that initiate Spirits' plan, guiding us to the right places at the right moment. It is all planned so that we may endure the challenges designed specifically for each soul, allowing us to learn lessons from Spirit. Hopefully, the assignment or chance meetings may come in many different ways, benefiting our soul positively, or negatively, depending on whether the occurrence comes in the virtues of love, happiness, or emotional pain. By not having much conscious memory of who we truly are, our Angels will help to navigate us back to our true selves if called upon. I'm very thankful for the assistance of my Guides because I would have continued to be a misplaced soul, continuing to make lower vibrational choices that would have kept me lost within the fallacy of life. Our Angels, under the direction of Spirit, help us to remember who we truly are by constantly communicating with us. They bring messages to us by way of our intuition, dreams, people, or even from a book or a song. Messages of love, danger, or fear are constantly reminding us of the reason we came to the planet. If we pay close attention to the assistance given to us, we can obtain an understanding that could help make the world a better place. By bringing us back to our true essence.

Being aware that we are given the power of choice depends on what we are creating. It's either going to be a pleasurable life filled with love and purpose, creating heaven on earth, or one of pain and difficulty that's caught up in a selfish life, orchestrated by the endless cycle of choices made from the ego. I realized that no matter how difficult my life situation may be, all I have to do is to self-reflect back to when I made the choice that had gotten me into a predicament. I am confident that I was given a warning from my Angels in some aspect before the choice was made. I discern the warnings or guidance by asking myself, how was the direction delivered? Did I have an uncomfortable feeling or thought about it? Did it come from a total stranger who gave me answers to the question I desired? When I start my day, I habitually call on Spirit to direct my steps, and I ask my Guides to assist me. They are here to do God's bidding by assisting us. They communicate with us all the time, we just need to listen in between the silence and follow their lead. Our Guide's spiritual sight into our lives is much better than we could ever see. When called upon, their assistance can help to propel us towards a life filled with love, joy, good health, and happiness, but most of all, being in service to the Source of our existence and others. They are to liberate souls by enabling them to create and experience an amazing life, bringing heaven on earth.

CHAPTER 11
LIVING AND CREATING LIFE AS YOUR TRUE SELF

"Verily verily I say unto you, He that believes in me, the works that I do shall he do also." —John 14:12

When I wake up in the morning, one of the first things I do to start my day is to give thanks to God for life. I get on my yoga mat, pray, stretch, and do breathing exercises while holding specific body postures, ending it with a twenty-minute meditation. Then I go to the bathroom to take a shower, and while bathing, I'm repeating positive affirmations. One day I noticed that every time I entered the subway to take the train, I would sometimes, mostly unaware, mentally repeat a silent prayer. As the train pulled into the station, I would thank the Angels for finding me a seat perfect just for me. As the train doors began to open, I could see that it was filled with passengers; after all, what did I expect? I should have predicted it being in a New York City subway. Soon after entering, I started to have doubts about the prayer I had just requested. I would infer to myself that I didn't believe that I was going to find a seat today. The train was too crowded, and I became aware that I was thinking negatively. I quickly interrupted my pessimistic reasoning by reversing my intentions back into an optimistic state of mind. My positive mindset was achieved by clearly expressing out loud what I was grateful for. I would begin by confessing my gratitude to my Angels, then I would start to visualize my seat while slowly moving through the crowded subway car. I tried to sense the area where I was being guided to an open seat, though, I didn't see any. I walked towards this space with the hopes of positioning myself in front of a seated passenger, wishing on the possibility that they may get off at the next stop while standing in front of them. As the subway stops rolled by, my hopes quickly started to fade. Until the passenger who was sitting in front of me unexpectedly stood up to get off. I was amazed at how effortlessly I was given the seat that I consciously manifested with my invocation.

This began to happen so frequently that I became mindful that I was willfully manifesting this experience. So, one day I decided that I was going to make this a daily habit, now that I was mindful of what I was doing. I was determined to have some fun with this exercise to see what I could willfully create with my intentions. I was reminded that we are always creating in our subconscious minds, but thoughts are only one level of creation. What most of us are not mindful of is the power of words. Whether we are speaking from a loving space or out of anger. It all depends on the energy placed behind the words that are going to reveal to our emotional state of mind. Collectively, this assists in bringing forth the consequence of our thoughts. Causing us to experience what we chose to manifest deliberately. But the question that puzzled me the most was: will it be energized by the power of love or anger? Without a doubt, whatever is propelled out into the universe will always return to the place from which it was created. When we are centered as our true selves while simultaneously experiencing only in the present moment, then and only then will we be able to intentionally create a better life for ourselves, and also a more promising world for others. This can be done by knowing who we are allowing to create and what's being constructed, is it our inner child or our ego that's the architect? We have to ask ourselves what thoughts we are sending out into the universe. Will these thoughts bring forth a more loving and joyous experience? Or an ordeal filled with disappointment?

As our true selves, our intentions are only driven by love that's free of the ego, but to know who you are, you must first know who you are not. Taking time to sit in silence to connect with your inner child will be achieved by going inward to this space daily, connecting in this silent place with your true essence. I made an area in my home where I go to have twenty-minute sessions of silence. By making time daily and quietly sitting, it helped me to silence the negative inner dialogue that continuously occupied my mind. Repetitively performing this practice assisted in creating gaps in between the silence. At the beginning of my practice, the gaps lasted for just a few seconds. But as I continued to practice sitting in my private peaceful place, the moments of silence grew each time I entered this quiet domain. One day, I discovered that it was a place where time didn't exist. A realm where I became one with the Source of our existence. The moment I connected to this peaceful feeling, I was certain that I had returned to my inner child self. The pure unconditional loving energy that's free of the ego. It's a power that's enveloped in nothing but pure love; our true essence.

I became encouraged when I obtained a deeper understanding when I embraced the meaning of Christ's words when he said, "I and my father are one."

In between the silence is where our inner child, the purest aspect of God, is reminded of why it chose to have this human experience, revealing more and more of our true essence by uncovering the mysteries and the wonders of the world. Consciously manifesting a more joyous life, rather than one filled with pain. As I continued to go within, I gained clarity by being able to discern where my self-imposed pain came from. I became cognizant that I made a lot of lower-level choices in my life. Most were made out of fear and not from a higher aspect: love. Once I became mindful of my thoughts, I decided to choose differently than what I previously understood to be the truth. Instead of continuing to believe in the falsehoods of my ego, I began to make choices that were formulated from positive patterns of thoughts. Implementing this change helped me to recognize life's falsehoods. However, the way to get to the truth was to allow the authentic part of me to lead the way. Recognizing this while existing in a positive state of mind, I knew that my truth would always come from love.

The more I was in this childlike innocence (unconditional pure love), the more I saw through the illusions of the egotistical world. Which at one time was all I thought existed. Fortunately, I gained an understanding of the truth that set me free from my mental and emotional blocks. These unrecognizable barriers were fallacies that I believed in for so long, unaware that these untruths existed within me. I was temporarily mentally ill by the self-inflicted negative thoughts of self that I had unconsciously believed in for so long. Injustices that were repeatedly committed by me because my ego had convinced me to believe that they were true. Unfortunately, those impressions clouded the hidden truths of my magnificence. Because I now understood the existence of my true essence, I wasn't going to be fooled again. I began to consciously create a better life by practicing staying in the highest vibration of love. So, I asked the Source for guidance, and I was given the wisdom to continue practicing my daily routine. This would keep me in the highest vibration, giving me the ability to be able to manifest my dreams. I was instructed from the minute I woke up, to the moment I went to sleep. I would constantly ask myself how I felt By asking myself this question daily, it would bring me back into the present moment. Doing this investigation would help in pulling me out of the grasp of the emotional bondage of my ego. If I'm constantly reliving an experience in my mind from the past, those memories will cause me to become entangled in negative thought patterns. These sentiments will cause an unfavorable emotional reaction that may emerge as a physical ailment or some other emotional characteristics, such as anger or depression.

I use this emotional technique as a gauge in assisting in reminding me to become aware of my thoughts. A place from which we all manifest in the present moment our experiences. By maintaining this awareness, I'm able to formulate a positive flow of energy deliberately directing it behind optimistic intentions. So, if I wanted to experience a day filled with favorable outcomes, all I had to do was focus my thoughts on what I would like to bring forth into the physical plane. Therefore, I would become emotionally excited about it as if I already obtained it. By occasionally daydreaming about it, it freed my inner child to willingly let go of my excitement. Every once in a while, I allowed myself to feel the enjoyment of it throughout the day. Once my goals were physically obtained, I would remove prior desires and replace them with new thoughts of my ambitions, once again placing them on my vision board. I remember to always be in a grateful state of mind because what I asked for has already been given by Spirit. I now walk with confidence knowing that we are all intrinsic beings, allotted the power to create a life filled with joy, love, and prosperity. Souls on a selfless journey yet always open to coming in contact with lost souls. Some wise and others not so sensibly aware. With the hopes that when we part, to be a blessing, not an affliction to one another. It all depends on the energy placed behind our thoughts, words, and deeds. Constantly being aware that what we cultivate in the world is going to determine what we are going to reap, but what we will leave with others. What we harvest will be from the highest vibration of love or the lowest pulse of our ego—which will it be?

I thought back to past mistakes I made when I allowed myself to succumb to my emotions. That stemmed from self-inflicted wounds created by choices not made from love, but instead rooted in the sins of my parents. As the saying goes, "when you know better, you do better," I gradually became more comfortable with how I managed my emotions. I knew that there was a big internal shift happening. I recognized that I remained in the flow of creation longer by becoming one with Spirit. Much to my surprise, it resulted in my day flowing at the highest vibration of love, enveloped in all of God's blessings that are created in the present moment of now where time doesn't exist. The more I continued to walk as my true self, it became easier for me to stay in alignment with the Source of our existence. It promised me the key to the doorway that will allow entrance to an experience so great, and a life filled with purpose and love, committed to being in service and a blessing to others. By assisting in freeing them from generations of mental bondage. Pointing them in the direction of the road of healing that I once took. The road less traveled where we could surrender ourselves to the Source of our existence. The one who could liberate us from the bondage of our ego and the sins of our parents. Emancipated to no longer suffer from a causeless cause by giving it a reason for its existence in our lives. Nonetheless, we begin to celebrate something much greater than man, a purpose much more magnificent. Giving honor to Spirit for a wonderful life that came to fruition. One we could never have dreamed of creating for ourselves. But if we could experience life's journey as our true selves, we will have the chance to experience life the way the Source of our existence conceived it to be.

CHAPTER 12
CONSCIOUSLY LIVING LIFE
WITH A PURPOSE

*"Two of the most important days of your life is the day that you were born,
and the day that you find out why." —Mark Twain*

In 2012, I was back in Cape Town, South Africa. I was looking
forward to meeting up with my spiritual teacher, an earthbound
angel with a beautiful heart. His only desire for me was to be happy
and protected, but the most important wish was for me to be in good
standing with my ancestors and God. It was during this return trip
back to Africa that Lwando Madasi had passed away; he had returned
to the Source of our existence, and my heart was crushed! I wondered
about why I was more emotional when he died than when my parents
had crossed over. There was something that felt different about this. I
recalled the day I went to visit Lwando in the hospital with my buddy,
Siv. When we arrived, I began questioning him about his health. As he
casually babbled on about how he was feeling, Lwando didn't explain
that he was having difficulties with his heart. Just as I was about to

interrogate him some more about his condition, Siv interrupted, "Bernard read this." He insisted that I read Lwando's medical chart. As I glanced over it, I was a little perplexed by his desire for me to read it until my eyes arrived at the area where Siv's finger was pointing. It read '*write the name of a family member in case of an emergency*', and written on that line was my name and number. Siv and I both raised our eyes and stared at Lwando with a lot of love and sympathy. I was deeply touched and saddened because at that moment, I realized that he was truly alone without a family.

As I continued to reminisce about our friendship, I recalled the day I invited him to my place to eat a warm cooked meal. While preparing the food, we conversed about several different subjects. I always enjoyed listening to Lwando because his intellect was deeply informative and wise. I noticed that he had stopped speaking because it had become silent. As I turned around, I caught sight of him silently staring at me.

Just as I was about to speak, he said, "Shame, your father is having a hard time on the other side, but he's a strong soul," while staring at his photo (my father had just passed away). Lwando continued, "Bernard, you are so powerful and don't even know it. Mario is weak [Mario kept succumbing to past regressions], but you haven't yet tapped into it, but when you do..."

Then he casually went back to where we had halted our conversation and continued where we left off. I wouldn't quite mentally grasp the profound meaning of that message until years later when it would be confirmed.

Another validation I received about Lwando's true identity was one night when I was walking home. I was on the main road that was one avenue over, parallel to the beach where Lwando slept. It was one in the morning, and I spotted him walking on the opposite side of the street. I shouted over to him, "What are you doing up so late?" As I crossed the street to approach him, I noticed that he didn't respond. With no expression, he just put one foot on the wall and leaned back into the position. As I was standing facing Lwando, a friend of his walked up to us. Lwando had previously introduced us a week ago.

Johannes was a white South African (anyone he introduced me to had something special about them, and there was some profound reason Lwando made the introduction) who had just come back from living in the United States. As Johannes approached, he stood in between Lwando and myself. Casually he turned towards Lwando and while staring at him stated, "Someone is about to get their wings."

I glanced at Lwando, but he didn't react. He just stood there with a blank expression on his face. Then Johannes turned towards me looking directly into my eyes, and he stated with a smile, "Oh I'm sorry you weren't supposed to know that." Suddenly, Johannes quickly said his goodbyes and walked off.

As I came back into the present moment, I discovered a tear rolling down my cheek while I reflected on the memories of my friend. I recalled him saying to me, "You're going to speak about me a lot." And my response was that I already do. While shaking his head Lwando repeated, "No, you're going to speak about me a lot." As the vivid memory faded away, I thought to myself, *You were right my friend, I will forever speak about meeting an earthbound Angel.* I inhaled then exhaled, my eyes focused on the setting sun. My heart spoke and confessed that I missed my friend. As I continued watching the vanishing sunset, the memory of Lwando also began to fade. I began to feel in my spirit that my return back to Cape Town would be different than the previous trips.

My boy Mario had left and was back in Angola. He was now the proud father of two beautiful children. Due to his suggestion of me becoming a vegetarian, I was now living a much healthier life for the past four years free of alcohol and meat. I now only listened to my body's request to retain or discard certain foods. This produced a much healthier body by only living according to what it yearned for, so I was a happy vegetarian. I had taken a happiness, breathing, and meditation course with The Art of Living. I diligently performed my practice twice a day, every day, for the past four years. I was so disciplined that I only missed four days of practice during those years due to my travels. Having successfully reconnected with my inner child, I continued to go deeper by doing the soul work needed to heal myself.

I begin to unravel more of who I truly was by recognizing my blocks. I learned how to release them with love during the process as my soul healed. When I began to connect deeper with Spirit, a transformation took place. One day I was finally able to truly say and feel that I loved who I was. My self-love grew by halting the false impressions of my ego that created the spiritual blocks. Once I had gotten a glimpse of my true self, I began to consciously exist as such, henceforth not believing otherwise. I now knew the power that I possessed within. As my true self, I was able to experience and manifest a wonderful life. Experiencing it as some of the ascendant masters in the past had achieved. They mastered the art of living by seeing through the illusion of the world. The more I stayed centered, the more I was able to uncover the truth. But I still had a lot of work to do. I was unaware of the spiritual events that were soon to come. Circumstances that would forever change my life. A profound encounter with God would soon give me the answers to the many questions about my life's purpose.

It was a sunny beautiful day with blue skies in Cape Town, and I had decided to go see a friend of mine. Yursa was this tall, beautiful, half Jamaican and Nigerian British model and actress. We had both previously acted in a film where we played husband and wife. As I entered her home, she introduced me to her girlfriend who was visiting with a friend of hers. When I saw Konya's face, it looked very familiar to me, so I asked, "Don't I know you?"

She explained, "No, we haven't met before. I just arrived in Cape Town from Johannesburg with a friend of mine, PK." I continued staring at her because deep within my being I felt as if I knew her. Yursa was making lunch for them, and as she continued preparing the meal, she informed me that PK and Konya had been kicked out of Kanya's father's house, who happens to be an ambassador.

They were looking for a place to live as at the moment they were homeless. For a split second, a thought came to me, *Maybe I should let them stay at my place?* Yursa was sharing a house with three roommates, so she couldn't let both of them stay in her room. I was going to have to pray for guidance because the last person I let stay with me wasn't the easiest person to live with. They also weren't grateful for the accommodation that was provided free of charge. I decided to keep my thoughts to myself, so I didn't offer to lodge them. I did try to encourage them by expressing to them that their circumstances would change, just have faith. I shared with them some of my own experiences during my travels, and at the end of it all, everything always worked out. I began to smell the aroma of the food Yursa was cooking, and I began to get a little hungry. Being a vegetarian, I knew that I couldn't eat what she was preparing, so I decided to step out to get something to eat.

When I returned, Kanya and I sat in the living room on the sofas across from each other. We conversed a little bit, but as I stood up to leave and say my goodbyes, I heard Kanya say, "Bernard! I have something to tell you." It wasn't what she said but how she said it was what piqued my curiosity. Her voice resonated deep within my soul that I was able to hear in between the silence to know that the voice came from deep within her being. I felt as if I had heard this voice before; it seemed familiar to me, and I didn't understand why. So, I sat back down and leaned forward, and with discernment, I listened intently to what Kanya was saying.

She continued, "Bernard, all your ancestors are here. They are so proud of you, and they want you to know that they love you, but you must pray and do a meditation. Your mother wants to show you something." Konya repeated, "They want you to pray and do a meditation. Your mom said she is so proud of you. But when you do this meditation, she wants me to be present."

My response to Konya was that I'd have to pray and sleep on this, and that I'd call tomorrow with an answer. Again, I got up, said my goodbyes and left. As I made my way home, I reflected on all that was disclosed to me. I thought to myself, *How did she know that my mother was deceased?* As what I had just experienced sank in, I became deeply moved.

The following day I woke up so tired that I didn't do my prayer and breathing exercises, not even a little yoga. This wasn't the norm for me to skip my daily practice. I had to do some type of training, so I changed my barber's appointment to noon and rushed to the gym. I wanted to get a haircut before I went on this Canada Dry commercial casting for the US. I had made up my mind and decided to do the meditation my mother had requested. I called Kanya to confirm if we were still on to meet at my place at 8 PM. She gave a definitive "yes." I then asked if we could change the time and make it earlier because I was shooting the next day at 6 AM. She again replied in a voice that was strong and direct, "8 o'clock."

I laughed and sarcastically said, "Ok, come with the whole crew!"

We met at my place at 8 PM sharp. I wondered what my mother could possibly want to show me. It had been many years since she had passed on, and I had many questions. Could she still be with me? Let alone all my other ancestors who had also crossed over. I was curious to know why they said that they were proud of me. Have they been able to observe my life and my choices? Suddenly, I had a flashback to the day that I first met Lwando walking along the boardwalk, and one of the first things he said to me as he walked towards me was that my "ancestors [were] not happy" with me. I thought to myself, *I must be doing something right because at the moment they must be pleased with me?*

Kanya and I prepared ourselves for the meditation by starting with a prayer, then we took slow, deep breaths. Unexpectedly, I saw myself on top of a mountain wearing a white robe, sitting in the lotus position (a crossed leg position with the feet resting on the thighs) in-front of a fire. I reached into the fire and pulled out a long red robe. Down at the foot of the mountain, I saw a very muscular man, and a woman carrying a chest filled with gold, coming towards the mountain I was meditating on. I came down from the mountains and met them on a skinny, golden pathway. These ancestors (I was made aware that this ancestor was the only male allowed to be present because in his past physical life, he attempted to break the sins of our ancestors, but he wasn't strong enough or chosen to be the one to do so) that stood before me were very attractive and tall. What was also surprising was that they were extremely well built with curly light hair. They permitted me to walk ahead of them down this golden pathway towards a cave. I entered the entrance of the burrow and they followed. Suddenly I saw a group of women all wearing red robes, and they were on their knees chanting and praying in the dark. As I walked further into the cave, moving through the crowd of women, they cleared a path for me with every step I took. I was a giant, much taller than they were. The women carried a golden throne to the far end of the cave and motioned for me to sit. As I sat down on the throne, they all got on their knees and bowed down with their heads touching the ground towards my direction. The man and the woman who carried the golden chest sat it down in front of me.

Suddenly, there was a big flash of white light that shined brightly behind me from where I sat. It filled the whole cave and cleansed it. Then green vegetation began to grow all around us, and the cave began to glow. The darkness that exited was expelled by an emanating green light. My ancestors had a message for me, they said, "You won't have to struggle, you will be guided and speak from your heart, that energy will help guide you to plant the seeds of freedom in others." At that moment I was filled with so much love. They resumed, "Now your work begins, we have paved the spiritual road for you, but you have done the work in conquering your blocks. Those blocks would have prevented you from connecting to your spiritual path—your destiny." Within a flash, I saw in my mind's eye some more of my ancestors out in this beautiful meadow. I could see them staring in the direction of the cave where the events had just taken place. In a flicker of my mind's eye, I saw myself walking through the crowd where my ancestors were gathered. My grandmother had her head held downward while clenching my mother's hand (I saw my mother quickly regress from an adult to a child); she had to walk in humiliation amongst our ancestors while the many generations of forefathers stood in line staring at my grandmother. She had to exhibit her regret and shame that was brought upon the family.

My grandmother for some reason made the decision not to believe or support her daughter when she confided in her that she was being molested by family members. Supposedly, my grandmother didn't address the situation, but chose instead to act as if the abuse never happened. The next vision I saw was my grandmother and mother entering this hut. My mother (as a child) laid down on what appeared to be a bed. My grandmother pulled the covers over her child as if she was tucking her in for bed. Hence, I saw this bright white light underneath the covers. At that moment, I knew in my spirit that my mother was finally at peace. However, the sins that had cursed the women in the family were what kept them in some form of bondage. These sins lingered amongst others in my family for generations, brought upon them because of the choice of no action by my grandmother. She chose not to protect her daughter by speaking out, but fortunately, it was now mended. As I began to come out of the meditation, I understood that God had chosen me to see what sins were committed in the past. I emerged from the experience asking myself, *Were there other family sins existing that were being passed down to another generation?*

I pondered on that question while writing this chapter. Then I remembered a family member whose husband was abusive to her over the years. I'm sure there were times when she may have thought about leaving with her two young sons, but never did. Why would she choose to stay in the marriage? As the years passed, she became an amazing, involved, caring, and fiercely protective mother. With two very intelligent college-educated, business-minded young men. However, because she never removed them from that toxic environment when they were children, I can see how her sons have been mentally, physically, and spiritually affected. Did I suspect that along our generational lineage there must have been someone that may have been abused or the abuser? So, I did some inquiring, and unfortunately, I didn't have to look very far. The man that I was close to growing up who acted out of character when he drank was my grandfather. I discovered that he was physically and or verbally abusive to my grandmother (my mother's father) when he was intoxicated.

I got an epiphany as to why God allowed my mother to show me not only the sins of my grandmother, but the sins of my mother as well. I came to understand that my mother's sin was that she told no one that she was sexually abused as she may have only confided in her mother. Instead, my mom chose to internalize it by blaming herself instead of conveying her story. If my mom would have shared her story, it could have possibly healed her by assisting in freeing others from their pain? Instead, she chose to take it to her grave, never for it to be spoken about. It all started to make sense to me at an early age and into adulthood. My friends and total strangers would open up to me. Sharing their most intimate, painful ordeals they had experienced. Some of the stories shared by both males and females was that they were molested as a child. I had many people of all nationalities, ages, and ethnicities divulging their personal stories of abuse, no matter what country I was in. It began to happen so frequently that it came to be normal. Until one day I had to ask, *God, why were they confiding in me? Was I molested and couldn't recall that I was?* The insight I received was that my mother had soul agreements she didn't fulfill. Those who were abused were drawn to me. Though I wasn't aware of it, I was able to counsel or just to listen to other painful experiences. It helped to atone for my mother's sins enabling her soul to be at peace.

It was apparent to me that each life has purpose and importance. What makes our existence valuable are the agreements made with God before we are physically born. So, when we cross paths with souls, we should try to leave each other with an experience that helps us along our life's journey. Support of some kind so that our souls may be healed and awakened by love. Our higher conscious self knows that when a soul's paths cross with another that it was destined. In your heart, you know that miracles can take place if we so choose, with God's guidance. Souls are assisted because they asked for help and received it. Our fundamental reason for living is to serve others with love, and by doing this, we serve God. So, when I start my day, I pray and repeat positive affirmations; this always raises me into the positive vibrational frequency of love. Vibrating at this level is the highest level to reach, for love is God. I became aware that once I began to walk as my compass to God, I was vibrating at a higher level. Not only did I attract others vibrating at that level and living as their true selves, but I was also tested by other souls vibrating at a lower pulsation. Fortunately, most of the time I didn't allow those experiences to knock me out of a loving vibration. If I did become uncentered by lower energy thinkers, I would realign myself by imagining how my day would be if I was experiencing it as my inner child. Our compass to God, the inner child, will always guide us to experience a phenomenal life. Just by asking a simple question, *God, what would you have me to do?* Call upon your Angels to assist in guiding you to be at the right places and at the right time, enabling you to manifest an amazing loving life the way God intended it to be.

Living consciously gives us the power and clarity to make higher-level choices. Bring forth more positive consequences that affect not only our lives, but others' also. It's much better to follow our inner child and make higher-level choices than make lower-level ones from the ego. The decision made by the ego only brings us temporary joy and pleasure, later giving rise to nothing but difficulty and sorrow that creates obstacles in our lives that keep us from our blessings. But when we consciously walk as our true selves always being centered in love, then, and only then will we be able to pass the torch of love, to light the way, freeing us all from past soul ties. Enabling us to see the purpose of the illuminated path, so that we may return to love to be enveloped with the only truth of all, for the only truth is love, which is God.

My Mom in 1988, the year before she passed

CHAPTER 13
LEGACY OF LOVE

"Train up a child in the way he should go: and when he is old, he will not depart from it." —Proverbs 22:6

It was a beautiful summer's day and I had just arrived home, and as I walked up the stairs to the front porch, I tried to enter the front door, but it was locked. There was a house rule that if we were sitting or entertaining in the backyard, the front screen door should always be locked. So, I descended the stairs of the porch to walk around to the back door. As I entered the door, I encountered my mother standing two steps above me in the kitchen. She seemed to be very excited about something and couldn't contain her emotions, so she began to share it with me. "Bernard, I had a dream that I was going to meet a man that was a Bishop, and I was going to be very happy." She was still smiling and barely able to contain her excitement about what was to come. My response was, "Mama that's great! You deserve to be happy, I can't wait until you meet him."

She smiled and descended the stairs from the kitchen, and as she passed me to exit into the backyard where her guest was sitting, she put her hand on my shoulders and said, "Me too." I walked into the kitchen to look out the back window to see my mother speaking with the visitor. I thought to myself, *God let this come to pass* (at that time, segments of my mother's life would not be revealed to me until many years later) *because she deserves to be happy.*

Six months later, the prophetic dream that my mother had would be fulfilled in a way that she nor I would have never imagined. One morning, I was abruptly awakened out of a dream by a big flash of light. As my heart was thumping, I wondered what was causing it to react that way. Like my mom, I too was a dreamer, and after having them, I needed to obtain a deeper understanding. So, I would seek her understanding of them because she was a much better interpreter than I was. It was a Saturday morning on a cold winter's day; I had drunk at a party I attended the night before. It was difficult for me to get out of bed, so while lying there, I pondered about the dream that I was abruptly awakened out of. I could hear my mother in the hallway closet, and I thought about how I couldn't wait to tell her about the dream I just had. I decided that I would tell her that night when we were both at home. I could hear her preparing herself for work, which was odd because she never worked on weekends, and neither did I.

I was twenty-three years old and was working as a high school mediation case counselor, so I had to get up and go to the high school to do mediation training with the students. At the very end of the training, I was sitting at a conference table and suddenly felt this pain in my head. I clasped my head with my hands and for some reason, I looked up at the clock; it was four-thirty. I didn't think much about it because I just thought that maybe I needed to drink water. After the training I was dropped off in front of my house by the director of the program. One of my sisters came rushing to the car, so I rolled down the window and she said, "Bernie, Mama was rushed to the hospital, she had a stroke." As I exited the car, dumbfounded, I asked, "When did this happen?" Her response was, "About four or four-thirty." All I could say was, "Wow."

After my mom's funeral, I realize that she must have known that she was about to cross over. I thought back to a particular day that I recalled leaving my room to go downstairs to get something to eat. When descending the stairs, I passed my mom's bedroom and I overheard her say, "This is the first time in my life that I'm caught up with all my bills." Not only were her bills in order, but we also found on her nightstand insurance paper and a letter to God. The letter thanked Him for the blessings each of her children received the year prior, considering that we were only one month into the New Year, we had no idea that two weeks later she would be gone. I believe that every soul subconsciously knows when they are going to physically die. I now know that the dream I had the night before her stroke showed me the very near future of my mother's passing. God must have known that it was too much for me to handle. So, a big flash of white light was used to wipe away the memory of what I was shown, but my heart knew what was to come. Years later, I began to comprehend the reason why her stay on this planet had to be a short one. My godmother stated that I would have been restricted in my spiritual growth because I had my mom to go to for answers, but now I turn towards God.

I truly believe that we choose our parents, and the union between the two bring in a lifetime of experiences. Each one of them brings into the relationship two separate experiences. One parent, if not both, may have had more of a traumatic ordeal than the other. Affecting not only their individual lives, but that of their families. The divine plan brings together souls by placing them with particular parents; within the same soul groups constructed for spiritual expansion. Though I wasn't close to my father, I'm now able to sift through his childhood traumas and ego to recognize the spiritual gifts he possessed. In which he may have knowingly or unknowingly transferred to my siblings and me.

My mom, she was the parent who instilled a strong foundation of love in our family. At the age of three, I recall pretending that I had fallen asleep in the chair, and my mom would come to my rescue. She would pick me up, lay my head on her shoulder, and carry me to bed. As she was carrying me to bed, I would open my eyes and see my brothers staring at me because they knew that I was faking it. I would do this from time to time just to get her attention and love that I longed for. Even if just for a few minutes. After all, she did have seven other children to attend to, let alone having her own life to live. I can say that my mother never once exhibited favoritism towards any of her children; she equally expressed her love towards all eight of us. Sometimes I would catch my mother lost in thought, and I often wonder what emotional memory was tugging at her heart.

Our home was welcome to all, whomever we brought home my mother received with open arms no matter the race. Whatever troubles a visitor was carrying; the doormat should have read "leave all your worries at this home." Because when they parted her open arms and heart, they left feeling as if they were family. We didn't have very much, but whatever we did have my mother shared. Three times a year, my mom and her brother would go to the butcher, choose a pig, and have it slaughtered for it to be barbecued on the barbecue pit in our backyard. My uncle Jun would methodically clean and prepare the pig with his homemade seasonings, spreading it all over the pig throughout the lengthy cooking process. My uncle would begin the process at midnight, well into the early morning hours. Anthony and I were two excited young kids wanting to take part in the process. So, we would sleep on the lawn chairs in the backyard imagining that we were camping under the stars. Then when the festivities commenced, my mother would open the invitation to the whole neighborhood. How she fed everyone is a mystery to me.

At fifteen, I was a young, opinionated, ambitious high school freshman. One day I was in my room watching television and became annoyed by what I was seeing. I began speaking out loud directing it towards the television saying, "What is this I'm seeing?" It was a detergent commercial, and at that moment my mother was standing at my door trying to figure out what was making her son so upset. I turned to her with my arms extended while pointing towards the television screen and I asked, "Mama, why is it that when they show a white couple washing their clothes, they show them in a house, but when they show the black family, they show the mother in the basement of an apartment building? Why can't they show the black mother in a house—we live in one?" My mother's response was, "I didn't teach you to be prejudiced." I said, "Mama, I'm not prejudiced, I'm just proud to be a young black man."

She stared at me for a few seconds, turned away from my doorway, then walked down the stairs without responding. Though, my mother was aware of the negative subliminal messages and images constantly projected about minorities. I believe that she could perceive how my ego could potentially mold my young mind into becoming prejudiced towards a certain group of people. Because of the boldness and insensitivity of the advertisers, they continue to perpetuate the subtle demeaning images. That is having a profound pessimistic effect on specific minority groups. Sometimes silence can be a very effective tool, and my mom had the wisdom to masterfully know exactly when to use it. Her calmness guided me to always reevaluate my thoughts and emotions when it came to someone else's actions and words. This became a useful tool to use as I matured in life. My mom raised my siblings and me to always keep your door open for someone in need. We were also taught not to judge anyone by the color of their skin, culture, religion, or economic situation. Instead, pray for them, and God would do the rest. Be proud of who God made you to be, and when you walk into these different circles of importance in life, walk with your head held high. Also, never believe that you are superior to anyone because we are all God's children.

One day I arrived home after attending an acting audition with a friend of mine. As I sat there with Franco observing the actors and the acting process; at that time I wasn't aware that I was interested in that world. I was expectantly asked by the casting agent, "Have you filled out the form to be seen?"

I replied that I wasn't an actor, that I was just here to support a friend, and she looked at me with a strange look on her face and continued signing in the actors. When I arrived home, I went upstairs to my room, and who did I see sitting on my bed, my mother. It was very strange to see her watching television in my room when she had one in hers. As I stood in my doorway staring at her, she was clapping with her arms above her head repeating over and over, "Beautiful! Beautiful!" because the actress, Vanessa Williams, had just won an award. Suddenly she stood up and turned towards me pointing in my direction while exclaiming, "And when you make it, you better thank God and Reverend James." The strange actions I was witnessing of my mother since I had arrived home mysteriously ended the way it started. Silence fell between us for a few seconds as she walked past me to go downstairs to her bedroom, still in a celebratory mood. She yelled out again, "Beautiful." I continued standing in the doorway feeling a little bewildered by what had just taken place. I questioned myself because how could she have known that I had just come from an audition, and because of that experience, I now was bitten by the acting bug?

My siblings and I today continue to ask: how did Mama do it? She defied the odds of being a single mom raising eight children. The statistical stigma for single parents in households, in particular that's run by black mothers bringing up black males, is pretty bleak. But I question these statistics because that's not what I experienced or saw within the black community; I see more triumphant stories. Four of my mother's eight children are males, yet she was able to form a healthy loving relationship with her sons. How was she able not to have her sons become followers, preventing them from getting caught up in the world and ending up in prison? As I look back on my life, my mother had the wisdom to know how far she could raise her male children, because a woman cannot make a man. She must've hoped that by raising her children in a middle-class neighborhood around positive black males that they would become role models to her son's, because they were raising well-mannered children themselves while nurturing their dreams. I thought back to the day my car was being repaired, so my neighbor Mr. Blount, the husband and father of four children, three males and a girl., offered to provide transportation for me to get home after I finished working at the High School. For the next few days until my car was repaired, I would meet him at his company. Mr. Blount was a successful, self-owned businessman. On the last day of his kindness, we were having good conversations about many different topics. This made the drive seem to have existed outside of the realm of reality because we had arrived at our destination so quickly. Before exiting the car, I thanked him for his assistance, then he said to me, "Bernard, your mother did a great job raising you guys." I was deeply moved because Mr. Blount grew up in an orphanage and foster homes. I was told that he never got to know who his biological parents were, or if he had any siblings. So, to have him express his admiration for my mom's rearing of her children touched my heart. I was emotionally unstable because it had only been a few months since my mother had passed. I thanked him as I closed the door and walked away; my heart swelled with love and gratitude to God for the virtuous mother we had.

We continue to be amazed by how Mama achieved it? How did she raise eight children alone, and none of us ended up victims of the many pitfalls in life? We all agreed on one definitive answer without a question; the prayers of a mother is what shielded us from the dangers of the world. My eldest sister, Peggy, of all of my siblings has the most children, three. Her eldest son, Michael, is the first grandchild of my mom and the first college graduate. How proud would my Mom have been to see her eight children achieving academic excellence and succeeding in many ways. For example, her firstborn son who took great financial risk yet was able to support a wife and child by overseeing a business of his own and now to see grandsons and granddaughters with college degrees, traveling the world, teaching abroad and as entrepreneurs. These dreams are being fulfilled because of God answering the prayers of a mother and grandmother. The power of prayer and the love of the Creator were instilled in us from an early age. Up to the present day, it rules my life and each of my sibling's lives and households.

I awakened one morning reminiscing about a conversation I had the night before with someone. As I sat up on the edge of my bed, I recalled saying to that person that at the end of our lives all we leave behind are photos and memories. Most artists and the spiritually connected know that for the first few minutes when we awaken, our minds are free of thoughts, and that's when we can tap into a creative energy flow. That's also the time when we can listen in-between the silence and hear God.

That morning, deep within my spirit, I heard God say, "But to leave a legacy is more profound." At that moment, I realized that it is not about how many souls you crossed paths with, but what you leave them with when you part ways. That's what builds a legacy. My mother's journey is still having an impact on not only her children's lives, and our family's future generations but also the lives of others. I can see it in my nieces' and nephews' eyes when we talk about our mother. The woman who defied the odds because she was able to lay her burdens at the feet of the Source of our existence. Giving gratitude always because she knew it would be taken care of. I'm so grateful to have had a phenomenal woman as a mother. One who taught her children how to live by faith, and trust in a life written by God, not by man. A mother who from time to time may have made choices that caused her to veer off into the dark. Yet she never got lost because she always looked towards the light. When a person's legacy bends the road of their destiny and they both meet at the Col-de-Sac of life, it's here where they both become one and the legacy begins to tell the story of love.

Mama, I don't wish you and my other ancestors back in this world, because why cry for a soul set free? I have no more worries or sleepless nights, missing or wondering if you are ok. I am delighted to know that your soul is at peace, and that you are truly happy because you are forever grateful to be loved and united with the Bishop.

Father

Though you were never around.
I AM always here,
Though you never showed me the way into manhood
I AM the way.
Though you never lived up to be the man; the image that I
could mirror but stayed an enigma.
I AM you, your true essence, more than a reflection,
For you are an extension of me;
The child of the father in spirit, not of the flesh.
 I AM the great I AM- now Go forth.
I now know who I am and walk as a king.
For I now know who my father is and forever Shall be.

-Bernard Fisher

Love IS

Love is being able at every moment to be enveloped inside, and out with the one and only love– God
Love is truth in all forms for the only truth is love,
Love is knowing.
For love is knowing;
Not believing– that no matter what your present truth is,
Love IS.
~Bernard Fisher